THE INVESTOR PROTECTOR

The
Investor
Protector

STORIES *of* TRIUMPH
over FINANCIAL ADVISORS
Who LIE, CHEAT, *and*
STEAL

DAVID P. MEYER, ESQ.

LIONCREST
PUBLISHING

THE INVESTOR PROTECTOR

Stories of Triumph over Financial Advisors Who Lie, Cheat, and Steal

ISBN   978-1-5445-1735-3 *Hardcover*

        978-1-5445-1733-9 *Paperback*

        978-1-5445-1734-6 *Ebook*

For my wife, Melora, and my kids, Jake and Leah.

Contents

Disclaimer

What would a book written by a lawyer be without a disclaimer, right?

The material in this book is based on my more than 20 years' experience as a lawyer in the trenches fighting investment fraud on behalf of my clients who hired my law firm and me to recover their losses. The stories I share are real cases from my law firm. Where appropriate, and to comply with confidentiality requirements, I generally do not use the parties' real names. In the few instances that I do include identifiable information about specific parties in jury verdicts and arbitration cases and the amounts recovered in disputes against particular brokers, the information is independently available in the public records and not separately covered by a confidentiality agreement. Prior results in cases shared in this book do not guarantee a similar outcome in any other case.

The information in this book concerning the securities industry, licenses, legislation, laws, regulatory records, and standards of care, among other topics, may change as legal and regulatory developments occur.

This book is for informational and educational purposes only and is not legal advice. This book does not create an attorney-client relationship. If you need to consult with a lawyer, you should take the time to find the right lawyer for your individual case. Determining a need for legal services and choosing the right lawyer are extremely important decisions. Do not base your decision to hire a lawyer solely on advertising. You should not take any action or decline to take any action in a legal matter based on the material in this book without first obtaining one-on-one advice from a properly licensed and qualified lawyer.

David P. Meyer, Esq.
Meyer Wilson Co., LPA
www.investorclaims.com

Foreword

ATTORNEY DOUGLAS S. ROBERTS

I first met David Meyer more than 25 years ago when I hired him as my law clerk. He was in his second year of law school and eager to get a taste of what it was like to practice law. At the time, I was working in a fairly large firm, specializing in personal injury and commercial litigation. We worked long days and dedicated hours upon hours to our clients.

The practice of law is not for everyone. It can be a hard way to make a living, but David quickly adapted to the culture of the firm. He was young, eager to learn, and a quick study. David also had a fearlessness about him that I admired.

When David graduated from law school, I gave him his first job recommendation. David was bright, hard-working, and eager to make his contribution to the world. When he left our firm, we were good friends. I told him to get as much trial experience as he could because you learn best when you are under fire. In my recommendation, I said that David would make a fine lawyer.

I was so wrong. In the years to come, David became not only a fine lawyer but a *great* one. He was able to do this because he discovered his passion for helping victims of investment fraud. When people discover their purpose in life, they are changed. They work harder. They are smarter, better prepared, and fight with intense courage. They are courageous, fueled by boundless energy. No one outworks them—no one. As warriors, they are unstoppable. And that proved to be the case with David.

Since the time he left our firm, David quickly earned a national reputation for successfully representing individual investors who are victims of investment fraud. I remember vividly nearly 20 years ago, as David's law practice was thriving, I received a copy of a business magazine and his picture was on the cover, with the title, "The Screwed Investors' Lawyer." I framed the magazine cover and hand-delivered it to his house. When David won his record-breaking $261 million jury verdict against Prudential Securities, I called him immediately and jokingly reminded him that when he started working for me as a law clerk, he didn't even know where the courthouse was.

I have seen the great work that David and his team have accomplished with my own eyes. It is no surprise to me that David has earned all the top national accolades and peer review endorsements (*The Best Lawyers in America*®, Lawyer of the Year, Super Lawyer, *U.S. News* Best Law Firms, Avvo 10/10, "A/V Preeminent Rating" from Martindale-Hubbell). I realize these awards and peer recognitions are important when considering who to hire, but David's personal character, empathy, and drive to help his clients are the factors that make him stand out in a crowd.

David speaks at seminars to lawyers and individual investors about investor protection. Much of the unimaginable harm caused by investment fraud can be prevented if one knows the right questions to ask before turning over one's life savings to a broker. To that end, David provides guidelines in this book to alert and protect us from becoming victims. The stories he shares in this book are revealing and the lessons we all can take away from them will make us more informed consumers who are better protected.

If I or anyone in my family were a victim of investment fraud, I would go to David for help. This is the highest compliment I can give.

Introduction

Meet Dorothy: She is 100 years old, sweet and assuming. She lives alone in a town near where she has lived most of her life.

Meet me: It's January 8, 2015. I'm an investment fraud lawyer attending a professional conference in Wyoming, trying mightily to get some work done. My plans change when I hear Dorothy's story, a story that involves small-town America, an invention, hard work, a life lived right, and $30 million. Dorothy's husband was an engineer who invented a critical piece of equipment for the government. He started a manufacturing company and, after 50 years, concluded his American Dream by retiring and selling his company. They relaxed into their retirement, secure in the knowledge that they had financial freedom for their family. Dorothy and her husband were conservative and never flaunted their wealth. At age 91, he passed away.

Meet the stockbroker: He works for a large national brokerage firm. He discovers Dorothy's financial net worth by befriending her adult daughter and pounces on the opportunity to pad his own pockets. Within six months, he swindles $30 million from Dorothy, almost the entire accumulation of the couple's life's work.

Back to me: A lawyer who heard me speak at a seminar a few years back calls and refers me to this case. No matter the amount, losing a lifetime of savings is devastating and life altering for victims *and* their families. After hearing Dorothy's story, I jump on a plane, and, two time zones later, I meet with Dorothy's estate lawyers and family representatives who explain Dorothy's distress and the ultimate goal of recovering her money before her passing. Challenge accepted.

This was a case that required all hands on deck at my law firm. We quickly drafted stacks of legal briefs for immediate court filing and coordinated a multi-pronged legal battle to take on several deep-pocket adversaries, who included three sophisticated defense lawyers from several law firms, including one of Wall Street's top defenders. In the end, I recovered $31,484,900.67 for Dorothy—more than $1 million more than she lost. A copy of the check (with the financial firm's name redacted for confidentiality purposes) is framed and hangs proudly in my office to remind me of the high stakes of the battles I fight for my clients. It's about the money, but it's also about the pride, retribution, and validation that comes with a hard-fought battle for what's right and just.

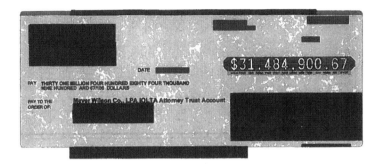

Finally, meet Dorothy's nephew: He calls a few months after the case settles to tell me that he has just returned from Dorothy's 101st birthday party. At the party, she asks him to thank me again for everything I did for their family. It's the best feeling in the world.

TRIAL BY FIRE

When I tell people I'm a trial lawyer, I say it proudly, fully understanding that their first reaction might be an internal eye roll. I get it. If your only experience with lawyers is based on what you see on television with cheesy advertisements, it's easy to believe the stereotypes. I'm proud of my profession. I've spent my entire career helping people up when they're down. I fight to level the playing field, restore financial security, and earn my clients the justice they deserve.

I'm your champion if you lose your life savings to an unscrupulous financial advisor—the last person you'd think would lie to you, cheat the system, or steal everything you've worked your entire life to save. While the majority of financial advisors and brokerage firms are good and honest, those who are bad and deceptive can ruin your life. I learned this early in my legal career. In fact, I was 28 when I filed my first investment fraud case.

While in law school, I was fortunate enough to work as a law clerk at a prominent personal injury law firm. I was mentored by great lawyers and experienced firsthand the hard work and long hours that come with being a successful trial lawyer. As I searched for my first position as an attorney, my boss recommended me to a small firm focused on tax and business law. In 1995, I started working at this firm while I completed my master's degree in tax law.

My stint as a tax lawyer lasted about two weeks because I just couldn't find a passion for it. The U.S. tax code, it turns out, is a boring read 10 hours a day. With the firm's business clients, I saw an opportunity in litigation, so I requested a transition from taxes to trial work. I dove in headfirst and was conducting jury and bench trials in the courtroom as a young lawyer. Flying solo and learning as I went, many of my nights were spent in the local law library watching videos of famous trial lawyers learning, among other skills, how to pick a jury, present opening statements, and cross-examine the opponent's experts.

You learn to be a good trial lawyer when you're thrown in the fire like I was. No matter the case, each one is unique and presents its own set of extraordinary challenges. I am a person who seeks challenges and thrives under pressure. In law school, I learned how to juggle clubs and fire torches and used them to procrastinate when I should have been studying. And even though I was never a distance runner as a kid, I picked up running and ran three marathons in my early years as a lawyer. I was also a professional whitewater rafting guide on the New River in West Virginia during my collegiate years. The New River includes extreme Class IV and V whitewater, and, as a guide, my job was to navigate a full boat of paying guests down the river and through narrow passages, steep drops, and huge waves. The job came with big responsibilities and big thrills. As I look back, it was the perfect training for a trial lawyer.

I've seen it all in the courtroom, from opposing counsel trying to punch me in the face after a pretrial conference to a lawyer having a heart attack in the middle of a jury trial during my cross-examination of his witness. In another case, a severe case of poison ivy the day before I started a jury trial forced me to wrap myself in Saran Wrap under my suit to cover the medical cream I'd applied all over my body for treatment. I squeaked when I walked, and the plastic peeked out of my dress shirt as I gave my opening statement to the jury.

Fortunately, my entire life I've been inspired in my pursuit of justice by a great lawyer: my dad. Still practicing after nearly 65 years in the small town where I grew up, he built his career helping victims of medical malpractice and personal injury find justice after life-altering events. My father's lifetime foes have been hospitals and big insurance companies. They could have been my foes, too, had an incredible opportunity not fallen into my lap as a green attorney a few years out of law school.

DAVID V. GOLIATH

Everything I learned about trial work in my early days armed me with valuable lessons that prepared me for my future. In 1998, three years after I completed law school, I led the fight on behalf of 300 families whose investment portfolios, worth tens of millions of dollars, were liquidated by one financial advisor at Prudential Securities. I filed the class-action lawsuit in which the majority of the class members were retired Whirlpool and GTE line workers with no investment or brokerage firm experience prior to their Prudential relationship. They trusted their advisor and Prudential with their life savings, unaware there was even a possibility their money was in the wrong hands.

I drove hundreds of miles to meet face-to-face with each one of the families I represented. I knew the names of their children, grandchildren, and even their pets. They were relying entirely on a verdict in their favor to recover their financial security. Their fear—and the weight of responsibility I felt—was undeniable.

We fought day and night for seven years against Prudential's army of Wall Street lawyers with their exceptional resumes, impressive track records, aggressive defense strategies, and seemingly unlimited resources. Many nights, I slept at the office, and my wife would bring me dinner and a change of clothes. We were certainly outgunned, but we would not be outworked. My team lacked the experience and bottomless wallets of our Wall Street opponents, but we made up for it with passion and commitment to make things right. I had to follow through on my promise to the families I represented that I would do everything in my power to get them the justice they deserved.

For the one-month jury trial, my team and I rented a local bed and breakfast and made it our temporary home base. When we weren't in court, we were there, often working more than 18 hours a day. My son was only seven months old at the time, and I was painfully aware that the sacrifices I made for my job impacted my family. To my entire team, though, this case was more than a job; it was a cause. Occasional visits home during breaks kept us going—that and a freezer in the bed and breakfast stocked to the brim with Klondike ice cream bars for late-night trial prep.

After a month in trial, many witnesses called to the stand,

and more ice cream bars than I'd care to admit, we had our result. The unanimous jury awarded our clients nearly $12 million in compensatory damages and $250 million in punitive damages. Winning a $262 million jury verdict at 32 was an incredible experience that I will remember my entire life.

To this day, the result of *Burns v. Prudential Securities* remains the largest jury verdict in Ohio's history. The appellate court reduced the punitive damages, but, in the end, we recovered $30 million with every family recovering more than 100 percent of their losses. They cried when the verdict was read. I cried when the verdict was read. Prudential's executives probably even cried but for very different reasons. From that moment on, I've been hooked: fighting investment fraud is my calling.

HUMBLE BEGINNINGS

My law firm has come a long way since I opened the doors as a solo practitioner back in 1999. Now, with seven lawyers and a robust legal support staff of paralegals and analysts, we have represented more than 1,000 investors over the past 20 years and have recovered hundreds of millions of dollars for our clients. But my beginnings were certainly humble. When I decided to leave my job and hang my own shingle as a young lawyer just a few years out of law school, it was just me and a small bank loan that I begged for. My former employer was gracious enough to rent me office space for a low rate. My wife and I went to a used furniture auction to get cheap office furniture. To this day, we still joke that she accidentally bid on a bunch of tables that we didn't need because she scratched her nose and inadvertently caught the attention of the auctioneer.

Most people thought I was crazy to leave my steady job and go out on my own to start a law firm focused solely on representing aggrieved investors against brokerage firms. Nobody I knew had ever done that. Many people asked how I was going to make a living by only taking investment fraud cases. Was I really going to turn down cases outside my area of the law? I knew I had to be brave enough to turn away other work so I could commit all my time and energy to investor claims. Ambition was a part of it, for sure, but it was more than that.

I felt fortunate as a young lawyer to discover a spark that combined my passion in this area of the law with a deep desire to build an innovative law firm on my own, from the ground up. I wanted to make a real and meaningful difference in people's lives. I didn't have family or business connections to lean on for help when I started. My wife and I lived on her salary as a high school English teacher for the first couple of years as I established my business.

I built my firm by hitting the pavement and talking to other lawyers, accountants, and other professional advisors to convince them, first, that their clients—victims of investment fraud—had legal recourse, and second, that I was the go-to attorney to help their clients recover their losses. I spent a lot of time driving around speaking at seminars about investment fraud. In the early years, I certainly had a full plate, between building my new firm and battling Prudential on behalf of the 250 retirees I represented during the seven-year-long class action.

I learned several traits early in my career which remain a bedrock of everything I stand for: to be compassionate, accessible, and authentic, and to understand there is no substitute for credibility. Most importantly, I always provide my clients with exceptional service.

BROKERS BREAKING BAD

That first big investment fraud case was legendary, and it set me up to take on Wall Street for the rest of my career. I learned that investment fraud is a serious threat to investors, specifically to retirees who depend on their savings to last them the rest of their lives. From the start of my legal career, I gained firsthand experience with the sophisticated and aggressive tactics utilized by Wall Street to defend cases brought against them. To make matters even more difficult for victims of investment fraud, a limited number of lawyers have significant experience handling these types of cases. For instance, the original Whirlpool retiree who brought his case to our office searched for months for legal representation before finding me.

Even now, my firm is one of a small number in the nation with a team of lawyers specifically dedicated to the niche practice area of representing investment fraud victims in cases against their financial advisors. Focusing on this area of law is a commitment that requires a robust legal team with exceptional expertise and plentiful resources to level the playing field against the army of experienced and well-funded Wall Street lawyers on the other side. Having decades of experience and inside knowledge of the financial industry is not a bonus for lawyers like us; it's imperative for consistent wins in these cases.

Our cases are not the kind you hear about frequently in the news, and the reason is simple: many victims of investment fraud never pursue their claims. Many don't even realize they are victims. They're often embarrassed. They blame themselves for trusting the person who turned on them. They think nothing can be done. Many only reach out to us after a friend, family member, or other trusted advisor becomes involved.

Often, victims of investment fraud don't even know they've lost their money. We've seen many deceitful brokers create fake account statements and hand deliver them to clients in their homes. Only when the scheme unravels do these investors learn that the amounts on their account statements had been false all along. The duplicity and dishonesty of bad brokers, combined with their willingness to steal from others and risk jail time, still amazes me after more than 20 years.

Bad financial advisors rely on a variety of factors for manipulation, but trust is by far their most important asset. The term "con man" is short for "confidence man," or someone who fosters confidence and trust, only to exploit that confidence for gain. Many investors believe they can trust their financial advisors because brokers are not typical salespeople—exactly as the financial industry wants it. Do you consider a car salesperson an advisor? Probably not. And you probably wouldn't invite them to your house for coffee every quarter to discuss your financial affairs. But this is exactly what investors do with their brokers. It's normal for us to entrust large sums of money to our financial advisors as "experts" without really knowing whom we're trusting or what they're doing with our money.

If you're planning for retirement or have already reached retirement, this is the minefield you face. Investing safely and prudently while maximizing your savings is not as simple as hiring any broker with a few good references.

My goal with this book is to alert you to potential pitfalls before you're a victim and to help you become a well-informed investor. If you've suffered losses at the hands of a bad broker, I want you to know that you have options. The right lawyer can help you win your fight.

My family learned the importance of finding the best professional to help solve a big problem when my son, Jake, a college swimmer, was diagnosed with thoracic outlet syndrome. A vein in the space between his collarbone and rib was compressed, blocking the blood flow from his arm back to his heart. The condition occurs with athletes who participate in sports with repetitive motions, such as swimming.

Jake's condition was serious and required surgery to clear a clot in the vein and remove part of a rib to release the compression on the vein. We needed to find a vascular surgeon who was well-versed in this condition and had experience performing this specific surgery.

The situation my family experienced is similar to what families experience when a loved one is a victim of investment fraud and needs to find the best expert to help recover their lost money. In my case, I was searching for a doctor in a very specialized area of medicine with many years of experience who had performed this exact surgery many times. I was looking for a doctor who was an authority in this area, had a strong team supporting him, and was genuinely invested in my son's care. The surgery had to be done right the first time—I wasn't going to chance my son's health on just any doctor willing to do the surgery.

In searching for an investment fraud lawyer to handle a case for a loved one, you need to focus on the same issues I was focusing on with my son. I wasn't going to allow an orthopedic doctor or a cardiologist to operate on my son. You don't want a divorce lawyer or a personal injury lawyer to handle your very specialized case of investment fraud. You have one chance to recover the money lost at the hands of a bad broker, and you need to find the best lawyer for your case who has the experience, notoriety, team, and resources to get the results you deserve. I did that for my son, and the surgery went well. I urge you to use the same diligence in your search for the right lawyer.

A BATTLE WORTH FIGHTING

After my first case, I continued to pursue investment fraud cases with a passion for helping financial fraud victims win back their hard-earned savings. In addition to assisting clients with the recovery of staggering financial loss, I conduct seminars and lectures on investment fraud and teach people how they can arm themselves against it. I make the time to provide education because I witness the emotional and financial damage caused by investment fraud and feel that no one should have to suffer through it.

Most financial advisors act ethically and keep their clients' goals at the forefront of the moves they make on their clients' behalf. But, as we've seen, some don't. Some see opportunities to profit from their misdeeds at the expense of unsuspecting clients.

I'm not a financial advisor, and I won't provide you with investment advice in this book. I will, however, show you how to protect yourself from investment fraud and what to do about it if it happens to you, a friend, or a loved one. This book isn't just for individual investors; it's for lawyers, accountants, and other trusted advisors who provide guidance and counseling to individual investors in their professional or personal lives. You are the frontlines of defense against this type of misconduct and often the first ones to spot a problem. Many of the clients we represent are referred to us by their attorney, CPA, or other trusted professional because they are often in the best position to identify red flags in their clients' investment accounts.

In Part 1, I'll discuss the complex framework of the financial services industry and the steps you *must* take before you hire a financial professional. If you follow the steps I outline, your chances of losing your life savings at the hands of a bad broker will reduce significantly.

In Part 2, I'll share with you the information I present in my seminars: how to minimize your chances of working with a bad broker, how to spot a possible fraudster, the warning signs that something could be wrong, and the most common types of investment misconduct I see in my line of work. You'll hear stories of investors I've had the privilege of representing throughout the last two decades. These are stories about smart, educated people who made the best decisions they could with the information they had, only to lose everything because the financial advisor they trusted turned on them.

Finally, in Part 3, I'll explain the critical criteria for evaluating and selecting the best investment fraud lawyer for your case. Wall Street has experienced and powerful attorneys on its side—so should you. I will also walk you through the steps involved in the legal process to recover your losses from investment misconduct.

Life is rarely simple, and it's sometimes unfair. This doesn't mean, though, that we give up when we face a hardship that seems impossible to overcome. People can help, and we have a legal process designed to right the wrongs and obtain proper justice.

You *can* make choices to protect your financial well-being. In fact, you've already taken the first step by picking up this book.

For starters, let's look at how the financial industry is designed and what you need to know before you hire a broker.

What You Need to Know Before You Invest

You've worked for many years, saved your money, and finally reached retirement or can see it on the horizon. You have trips to take, family to visit, hobbies to enjoy, and money to invest. Making money may seem like the hard part of your financial life. In reality, making your savings last—and keeping it—can be exceedingly difficult. The decisions you make *before* you entrust your money to a financial advisor help determine whether you spend the rest of your days enjoying your time with confidence and peace of mind or rebuilding your financial life.

The chapters in Part 1 will help you hire the right advisor. Before you decide *whom* to hire, it's important to understand *how* the financial industry is structured. It's complicated by design, but understanding a few key differences in the profession will put you leagues ahead of typical investors. This understanding is the first step in protecting your financial well-being.

Whether or not you've found a financial advisor to work with or you're just beginning the search, the tips and strategies presented in this part will help you on your path toward financial security.

CHAPTER 1

You Trust Your Broker—That's Good (and Bad)

Imagine that you're rear-ended at a stoplight and you sustain a moderate back injury. After calling the police, exchanging information with the driver who hit you, and visiting the hospital or your doctor for examination and treatment, what do you do next?

Most of us wouldn't hesitate to hire a lawyer to represent us with a personal injury claim. After all, why shouldn't we pursue damages for the physical injuries we endure because of the negligence of another?

But when the injuries are financial and the bad behavior

is not on the part of another driver but a financial advisor, research shows that most people with a meritorious legal claim never pursue it.

Why is this the case? Why would individuals allow a professional to lose, squander, or steal their hard-earned dollars, life savings, and lasting legacy? And if that money is lost as the result of someone else's misconduct, why don't they fight to get it back?

I'm a lawyer, not a psychologist. But after more than two decades representing the average individual investor, I've gained significant insight into the minds of victims of financial misconduct. It's clear to me that losing money and suffering a horrible violation of trust is a deeply personal and emotional experience for victims. Embarrassment and self-blame collide with fear; most people can't move past this conflict.

PROFILE OF AN AGGRIEVED INVESTOR

Many of my clients hold on to the shame and embarrassment of their broker's bad acts long after they learn what happened. They often feel defeated; they feel that somehow they could—maybe even should—have predicted that their advisor would engage in misconduct.

Other factors, including age, cognitive skills, and social

norms influence victims and their reluctance to talk about money. As an unsaid rule, talking about money is a taboo topic for many in American society.

If talking about money violates societal norms, then losing money can feel like the ultimate failure, especially if you're elderly, single, or widowed. Seniors with a lifetime of savings who possibly suffer from memory impairment or other debilitating conditions are frequent targets of greedy and manipulative brokers. These brokers know that their victims are lonely and vulnerable, living alone without trusted advisors or family nearby.

Take Gretta, for example. A former client referred to me three years after her husband died, Gretta lived by herself, was financially frugal, and relied on the broker her husband hired years before to manage the $2 million they saved. The broker was employed at a large Wall Street brokerage firm. Unfortunately, knowing that she was alone with sizeable savings, her broker saw an opportunity. He helped her with groceries and tended the lawn, frequently stopping by to make sure she had everything she needed. During these friendly visits, he also tricked Gretta into signing blank checks that he used to rob her of half a million dollars.

After she hired me, Gretta asked that I inform her kids about the case, as she was too embarrassed to share the details with them herself. Somehow, she felt it was her fault that the person she and her husband entrusted for years to guard their savings with sound, professional decisions had stolen from her. It was her fault, she thought, that he stole from her and manipulated her trust and their professional relationship, simply because he could.

To dislodge the shame and self-blame of my clients, my first step is to remind them that relying on experts to advise us in a specialized field is not a fault. We rely on our mechanic to tell us when we need new brakes and our accountants to prepare our taxes. Would it be reasonable to rely on your mechanic to render medical advice? No. But no one would fault you for relying on your doctor. And you likely wouldn't fault yourself if, for instance, the doctor gave you reckless advice that fell far below the standard of care and resulted in injury. If your injuries were serious, you wouldn't hesitate to take legal action.

The same must be true for financial professionals. We seek out and hire financial professionals because most of us do not have the expertise or the inclination to manage our own investments. It's complicated. The stakes are high. You don't have time or skills to study, learn, monitor, and manage your own investment portfolio. When things go horribly wrong because of a broker's actions, I make sure my clients understand that their trust was not misplaced. They're not stupid. They shouldn't have known better. The financial advisor and their brokerage firm should have known better—and there *is* something that can be done about it.

Once Gretta realized she wasn't at fault for losing her money, she decided to hold her broker responsible for his wrongdoing. We were able to recover all her lost money, regaining both her savings and a secure future. After we initiated our claim, the broker was charged by the criminal authorities with theft and ultimately sentenced to prison. My client felt relieved and vindicated at the end, but it was obviously very difficult for her to process the deceit by the broker she trusted for so many years.

The investment industry barrages investors with advertisements designed to elicit trust and comfort. You probably recognize slogans like, "With us, you're family," or, "We look out for your best interests." These promises should be real, but unfortunately, not all brokers are created equal and they don't always have your best interests in mind. People don't think they can lose their life savings at the hands of bad brokers because, between the industry titles and certifications and Wall Street's marketing efforts, investors believe they're protected.

No matter how much money you have, how smart you are, where you live, or what you've accomplished in your life, you can be a victim of investment fraud. I've represented professional athletes, entrepreneurs, doctors, lawyers, professors, and CEOs in cases against their financial advisors. I once represented a woman who initially contacted me from a payphone after surrendering all her property to a commune at the recommendation of her financial advisor. I have represented countless estates of deceased clients in which broker misconduct was only discovered when a distraught family member went through paperwork after the funeral. You can't typecast victims. Investment fraud can happen to anyone.

RIPE FOR THE PICKING

Life, with its 401(k)s, IRAs, and pension plans, can set us up as easy targets in our retirement years. In many ways, we're almost compelled to trust our brokers. During the 40 or more years we work, we spend little time managing the money that siphons into our retirement plans. While we certainly work hard to earn money and make sure we set it aside for our retirement years, the actual details of how it is invested are not something that many of us study. By design, we have little (if any) day-to-day interaction with our retirement investment accounts. We tend to focus on what's right in front of us, like jobs, kids, houses, pets, friendships, and aging parents. We necessarily prioritize these life happenings over the daily workings of our retirement accounts.

We meet with our 401(k) advisors occasionally, check a few boxes, sign documents, and ultimately allocate our money into a variety of different investment funds with little thought to the day we will actually use it. We repeat this cycle on a sporadic basis for decades, typically until our sixties or seventies when we celebrate the end of our working days.

We then enter a financial reality in which we have to spend without earning income from employment and rely on our savings for every expense for the rest of our lives.

The idea of living 20 or 30 years or more on a lump sum of money can be daunting, so it's no surprise that many of us seek income and moderate financial growth of that money in a safe manner. Most of us want to grow *and* protect our resources. We want our financial advisor to, first and foremost, manage our risk by recommending an appropriate investment portfolio based on our specific circumstances and implement the plan to generate income and moderate growth.

Unless you have prior experience with financial management or have a passion for learning about investing, you are in the majority of investors who need an advisor. You could open an account with an online brokerage firm, research options, invest money in index funds, and allocate it among equities and bonds to bypass the need for an advisor. Most of us, though, approach retirement with other priorities and prefer to delegate this responsibility to a trained financial professional.

It's normal practice for us to hire experts to handle matters requiring specialized training and skills. Investing is no different. Most of us (myself included) hire financial advisors to recommend and implement a sound strategy that meets our investment objectives and risk tolerance. With a law degree and master's degree in tax law, I sue brokers for a living and *still* entrust my savings to a financial advisor.

THE PEOPLE WE TRUST

Most brokers are honest, hardworking professionals who take their responsibilities very seriously. The small percentage of brokers who engage in misconduct, though, have ample opportunity to take advantage of their clients. The first step in protecting yourself is to diligently pick the right person backed by the right firm. The type of financial professional you hire makes a huge difference, both in the services they provide and the legal path you must navigate if something goes wrong. Selecting the right financial advisor is more difficult than you may think.

Most investors don't understand the structure of the financial industry or advisor registration. It's not your fault—the financial industry is purposefully opaque.

Many investors rely on the premise that their financial advisors are financially literate, well-educated professionals with expert training. Financial professionals use hundreds of professional designations with an alphabet soup of letters following their names to suggest they are particularly skilled in a certain area: AIF for Accredited Investment Fiduciary, CFA for Chartered Financial Analyst, CRFA for Certified Retirement Financial Advisor, for example. Some of these titles and certifications are legitimate; others are not. Unfortunately, the credentials some financial advisors use to "prove" their qualifications may be nothing more than dubious designations purchased for a few hundred dollars or "earned" with minimal effort.

While many designations (like the CFA and AIF) are serious credentials earned and used by competent, trustworthy advisors, some designations are not what they seem. Dubious designations can sound frustratingly similar to credible ones. Take, for example, CRFA. It sounds a lot like the CFA designation. The difference is approximately 900 hours of intensive study in accounting, economics, ethics, finance, and mathematics, in addition to a rigorous, three-part exam that only 42 percent of CFA candidates pass, according to the CFA Institute. The CRFA, by contrast, is earned by passing a multiple-choice test that doesn't require much preparation.

Properly licensed financial professionals fall into one of two categories:

1. Registered representative (also known colloquially as a stockbroker or broker)
2. Investment adviser representative

Sometimes, financial professionals are both registered representatives *and* investment adviser representatives, depending on the service they provide on a particular day.

THE LANGUAGE OF FINANCIAL PROFESSIONAL DESIGNATIONS

TECHNICAL TERM	WHAT IT MEANS	OTHER NAMES	WHOM THEY MUST ASSOCIATE	REQUIRED REGISTRATION	STANDARD OF CARE
Registered Representative	Someone who is licensed to buy and sell securities for clients and is sponsored by a firm registered with FINRA	Stockbroker Broker Financial Advisor*	Broker-Dealer or Brokerage Firm	FINRA	Best Interest
Investment Adviser Representative	Someone who engages in the business of providing investment advice for compensation	Investment Adviser Adviser	Investment Adviser or IA	State Regulator if Assets Under Management <$100MM SEC if Assets Under Management >$100MM	Fiduciary

*For decades, registered representatives were able to refer to themselves as "financial advisors," and it was widely used as a synonym. A new rule issued by the SEC went into effect on June 30, 2020, that prohibits registered representatives who are not also investment advisers from referring to themselves as "financial advisors."

When referring generally to individuals in the financial services industry, and when intentionally not distinguishing between a registered representative and an investment adviser, I will use the term "financial advisor" or "advisor" in the book.

REGISTERED REPRESENTATIVES

Registered representatives are stockbrokers who sell securities like stocks, bonds, and mutual funds. They are paid by commission on each sale. While the U.S. Securities & Exchange Commission (SEC) is the ultimate authority in most securities matters, the United States has significantly relied on a self-regulatory framework for brokers and brokerage firms. In other words, the financial services industry is expected to largely police itself.

Most day-to-day regulation of brokers and brokerage firms is handled by the Financial Industry Regulatory Authority (FINRA) rather than the SEC. FINRA is a self-regulatory organization that regulates brokers and brokerage firms. Every broker and every brokerage firm that sells securities *must* be registered with FINRA (with extremely rare exceptions). Registered representatives are required to work with a brokerage firm registered with FINRA to sell securities legally.

The United States has more than 600,000 registered representatives, and approximately 3,500 brokerage firms. Some brokerage firms, such as Merrill Lynch, Ameriprise, Raymond James, and Wells Fargo, are large enough to maintain custody of their customers' accounts. Other, smaller operations must use a custodian firm like Pershing or Charles Schwab to hold their customers' accounts and execute their transactions. FINRA regulates all of them. Should these firms violate industry rules or standards, FINRA can render fines, suspend them, or bar them from the industry.

I see registered representatives as salespeople because, everything considered, this is truly what they are. Their income is largely comprised of commissions from the products they sell to investors. Commission is the incentive for brokers. The more they sell, the more they make.

Many find it confusing that registered representatives have

referred to themselves as "financial advisors" for several decades. "Financial advisor" is a generic term with no precise industry definition. When we think of an advisor, we think of someone who offers unbiased advice and earns our trust with experience and training. We expect expertise, neutrality, and professionalism from our advisors. Yet somehow, almost every time I cross-examine registered representatives on the stand at an arbitration hearing, they deflect any sense of duty and instead refer to themselves as salespeople. The securities regulators addressed this confusion by enacting a new rule in 2020 prohibiting brokers from identifying themselves as advisors unless they are, in fact, investment advisers.[1]

What are the other rules and obligations of registered representatives? For starters, they cannot cheat, lie, or steal. Registered representatives cannot persuade you to buy or sell an investment by misrepresenting or omitting important facts. This includes providing investors with a long list of supposed benefits from an investment without adequately explaining the risks. "Boy, do I have a great investment for you," registered representatives might tell their client, stopping short of mentioning potential pitfalls. Maybe they fail to discuss illiquidity, or how commissions and fees cut into

---

1 Throughout this book, when referring specifically to registered representatives/ stockbrokers, I will typically use the term "broker." When referring specifically to registered investment advisers, I will use the phrase "investment adviser." And, despite a recent rule change by FINRA attempting to clarify the confusion in this area, when referring to individuals in the financial services industry in general throughout this book, I will use the term "financial advisor" or "advisor" since those terms have been used to refer to the profession generally for decades.

the investment's return. FINRA repeatedly states that brokers must provide a balanced overview of an investment—a challenging task for many salespeople. It's harder to make a sale if they have to detail the chance of significant losses and the true cost of what is being promoted, and for those reasons, those details are often not discussed.

In addition to being honest and upfront with customers, brokers have a specific obligation to act in the best interest of the customer at the time an investment recommendation is made.

Regulation Best Interest

The landscape of brokers' duties and responsibilities to their clients has changed over the last decade. Between 2015 and 2018, for instance, the United States Department of Labor (DOL) introduced, enacted, and then, under new administration in 2016, abandoned the Fiduciary Duty Rule, which would have mandated a fiduciary duty upon brokers working with retirement funds. The fiduciary duty is among the highest duties owed and is precisely the legal standard that many other investor advocates and I endorsed because, among other reasons, it's the standard by which most individual investors believe their financial advisors are bound. The back-and-forth that followed the death of the DOL's Fiduciary Duty Rule has given birth to a new SEC regulation called "Regulation Best Interest," or "Reg BI." According to the

SEC, Reg BI was enacted to enhance and clarify the standards of conduct applicable to brokers.

Implemented in June 2020, Reg BI expands the duties of brokerage firms from the old standard of "whether the investment is *suitable*" to a heightened standard of "whether the investment is in the customer's *best interest*." While that might sound like a fiduciary standard, it's a bit more complicated than that. The SEC has said that Reg BI "draws from key principles underlying fiduciary obligations" but stops short of assigning brokers an actual fiduciary duty. In my opinion, it doesn't advance investor protection because the regulation lacks clear definition.

Under Reg BI, brokers must understand their customers' life circumstances, investment objectives, risk tolerance, and other investment experience.[2] Next, they must match their recommendations with what they know about their customers. Is the investment recommendation the best fit for the investors' current ages, life circumstances, objectives, financial states, and risk tolerances? If it is, the brokers may have met their obligation under Regulation Best Interest. If it isn't, they have failed in their basic duties to their customer. While it shouldn't require a formal regulation to ensure that brokers work in the best interests of their customers, that

---

2   Reg BI also requires firms to provide customers with a document called a "Form CRS" that discloses information about the firm and the broker, including basic information about fees and conflicts of interest.

is how things stand in passing a directive in the securities industry in 2020.

This is the primary question I answer when evaluating potential claims against brokers: Did your broker recommend and implement an appropriate investment strategy suited to your best interests? If the investment was not appropriate and the investor suffered significant damages, both the broker and firm may be held liable for misconduct. It's important to mention that providing simple risk disclosures doesn't satisfy a broker's obligation to recommend an appropriate investment strategy, nor does it necessarily act in their customer's best interests. Selling securities is not like selling a used car—there's no "buyer beware" warning attached.

Sometimes, it's obvious that a recommended investment or investment strategy is completely inappropriate for a particular investor. If investors' life circumstances are such that they require conservative investments and their brokers sell them an entire portfolio of risky stocks, for example, the brokers' recommendations are obviously inappropriate and fail to meet the customers' best interests. Other times, though, the brokers must conduct a more careful analysis to determine whether a portfolio is appropriately allocated.

The duties of an investment adviser (versus a broker) are less ambiguous, easier to explain, and have been the same since the 1940s. Investment advisers have always been fiduciaries for their clients.

INVESTMENT ADVISERS

Investment advisers sell investment advice instead of an actual product. They do typically execute investment transactions for their clients, but instead of being paid per transaction and by commission, they are paid a fee for their advice that is often a percentage of the assets they manage or an hourly basis or flat fee. The important distinction to remember is that their compensation does not depend on executing transactions.

FINRA doesn't oversee investment advisers like they do registered representatives. Instead, investment advisers are regulated directly by the SEC or, if they manage less than $100 million in assets, by their state's securities regulator.

There are more than 13,000 investment advisers in this country, managing more than $83 trillion in assets. Investment advising is a booming industry, growing faster than the number of brokers in the FINRA world.

The Investment Advisers Act of 1940 imparts fiduciary duties onto all investment advisers. They must avoid conflicts of interest with clients and are prohibited from overreaching or taking unfair advantage of a client's trust. Fiduciaries owe their clients more than mere honesty and good faith alone; they must be sensitive to the conscious and unconscious possibility of providing less than disinterested advice.

In the landmark court decision in *Meinhard v. Salmon* in 1928, the overseeing judge, Justice Cardozo, stated:

> "A fiduciary is held to something stricter than the morals of the marketplace. Not honesty alone, but the punctilio of an honor the most sensitive, is then the standard of behavior."

Investment advisers are held to the highest standard with their clients. The standard of "suitable" and "best interest" recommendations in the broker world is elevated to the "fiduciary duty" standard in the investment adviser world.

It's important to know that, as explained earlier, both investment advisers and registered representatives may include a variety of different titles, complicating the process of selecting a financial advisor to manage your investments. Also, both can help you manage your financial health in additional ways, like assisting you with life insurance or keeping you updated on Medicare benefits.

Obviously, you need to look for more than a good name when hiring a financial advisor. We'll look at the credentials your advisor needs in Chapter 2, and how their credentials can make you feel better about investing.

Who Gets the Job?

When you need a new family physician, what is the set of criteria you follow to evaluate your options?

Maybe it's important to you to find a doctor within a certain mile radius of your home. Maybe you find one medical school more impressive than another, or you care most about the doctor's treatment philosophy. Among the variety of factors that help you select the right doctor for you, the primary criteria are most likely that an "MD," "DO," or another form of properly licensed medical credential follows their name. First and foremost, they must be a licensed, practicing medical professional to earn your trust.

Sometimes, you get lucky, and the first doctor available for your upcoming appointment meets all your criteria. As a general rule, however, the more time you spend researching your options, the better.

This "rule" applies to any professional advisor, including the men and women we trust with our investments. When it comes to your physical or financial health, a little legwork in advance gives you the peace of mind you need to move forward confidently.

I cannot recommend whether you should work with a broker or an investment adviser, but I can share with you the differences I've encountered representing investors for the past 20 years.

Every broker must be affiliated with a brokerage firm, or technically a "broker-dealer," to be in business. Broker-dealers have a unique set of duties and responsibilities to their customers. They have to carefully supervise their brokers to ensure that they are making appropriate investment recommendations and not lying, cheating, or stealing. If a broker engages in misconduct, the root of the misconduct is often because the broker-dealer was not adequately supervising its broker. In this instance, a broker-dealer can be held liable for negligence that results in damages to a customer.

Investment advisers have fiduciary obligations to do what's in their clients' best interests, often including taking steps to supervise their agents who manage money. Should an investment adviser breach these obligations, they can be held liable for negligence or breach of fiduciary duty.

Whether working with a broker or investment adviser, vastly different processes exist for pursuing legal claims if something goes wrong. We'll discuss these differences in Part 3. Suffice it to say that any dispute with a broker or FINRA broker-dealer lands in FINRA arbitration. Disputes against investment advisers, on the other hand, end up in arbitration forums or court, based on the specifications of the client agreement signed at the outset of the relationship. When deciding whether to hire a broker or an investment adviser, it may help to know that pursuing claims against brokers and brokerage firms is typically quicker and less expensive than bringing claims against investment advisers.

WHEN LINES BLUR

To make matters even more complicated, it's becoming increasingly popular for a financial advisor to be both a broker and an investment adviser. This creates a potential problem for investors: it's difficult for average investors to discern between their advisor's two roles and their two sets of obligations.

Your financial advisor may also recommend to you an insurance product, in addition to advice and investment. I've worked with several clients who bought inappropriate insurance products based on their broker's/investment adviser's/ insurance agent's recommendation. One of these clients was Mary, a 75-year-old widow who was convinced by her broker to purchase a whole-life insurance policy with a face value of $1 million that was issued by the brokerage firm's parent company and promised maximized assets.

However, the reality was very different from the promise. Ultimately, the exorbitant premiums and expenses of the policy caused Mary's accounts to be depleted by hundreds of thousands of dollars.

Mary's broker's recommendation included mutual funds, annuities, and life insurance. When she initially purchased the policy, her broker told her she was buying a single-premium policy (this means that only one premium would be required). Not only was this untrue, but the policy came with a hefty annual premium of nearly $80,000. These disguised premiums were paid by systematic withdrawals from annuities that the advisor had also sold to Mary, totaling nearly $250,000 in just over three years.

A few years later, Mary received premium notices in the mail because the annuities could no longer sustain the premium payments for the policy. When she inquired to her broker about the premium notices, he told her that she could disregard them because the dividends paid out by the policy more than covered the premiums. Unfortunately, this was also false.

Mary's broker had established premiums that were paid by an automatic loan feature within the policy contract. The dividends did not cover any premium payments but instead were added to the death benefit on the policy. The increase in death benefits, however, was effectively negated by the ballooning policy loan that was attributed to the unpaid premiums. To prevent the policy from lapsing, Mary was tricked into adding even more money into the policy under the guise of "stimulating growth," wholly unaware that the additional money was simply paying down the ever-growing policy loan.

After more than 10 years of being lied to, Mary met with a new financial advisor who told her the policy was unsustainable. She surrendered the policy and received a mere fraction of the nearly $600,000 in premiums she had paid into it.

The brokerage firm fought to have Mary's case dismissed and deny us the opportunity to present her case on merit. They insisted that they had no obligation to supervise the broker's sale of life insurance, explaining that when the broker sold the policy to Mary, he was acting as a licensed insurance agent for the insurance company. The three arbitrators appointed to Mary's case didn't buy it and denied the firm's motion to dismiss Mary's case. We settled the case shortly thereafter.

SIZE MATTERS

It matters that your broker works at a reputable firm with substantial resources for several reasons. First, a firm with resources can dedicate funds to its compliance and supervision responsibilities and be a more powerful watchdog in the handling of your life savings. Generally speaking, smaller firms typically have fewer financial resources to devote to compliance and supervision. Often, with a lack of sufficient oversight, these firms create a permissive atmosphere in which brokers can take advantage of their customers without getting caught—or punished—by their firms.

Conversely, larger brokerage and investment adviser firms theoretically have more substantial funds they can dedicate to compliance and supervision with the ability to hire more people, utilize more resources, and, hopefully, keep a better eye on their brokers. If a problem arises, you'll be in a much better position if the brokerage firm responsible for your losses has sufficient funds to pay you back in the event you prevail in an arbitration or court case.

Assume, for a minute, that you're ready to retire. You have $1 million from an employer-sponsored 401(k) to roll into an account with a broker-dealer of your choice. You've received referrals for brokers from your friends, and you've interviewed several people. The candidate you've selected—Brian—is good. You really clicked with him. He's charismatic, experienced, and promises to diligently protect your financial security. You're comfortable with this new relationship. In fact, you're excited. Why wouldn't you be?

Your first thought when hiring a broker is probably not to examine the worst-case scenario. But let's assume that the worst does happen. Maybe Brian's financial troubles run deep. He's the subject of several tax liens, and he's struggling to pay his bills. In desperation, Brian has moved all of his clients out of well-balanced, diversified portfolios and into risky alternative investments that pay him substantial commissions. He convinces you to invest your $1 million into an oil and gas private placement that will, he promises, pay steady and generous dividends.[3]

One month later, the oil market goes into turmoil and the company you invested in is not prepared to weather the storm. The company files bankruptcy, and your investment is now worthless. Your entire life savings is gone.

You likely have a good legal claim against Brian and his brokerage firm for selling you a wildly inappropriate investment recommendation, but will they be able to pay the claim if you prevail? This is a question you must ask yourself before you hire a broker and a problem arises.

---

3   Before you say, "I would never agree to do that!" think about how charismatic Brian is and how easy it would be to immediately trust him. We'll dive deeper into this dynamic in Part 2.

I once represented a labor union in losses it sustained in a massive, multi-state Ponzi scheme orchestrated by a financial advisor at a brokerage firm. The union had invested $725,000 in what it thought was FDIC-insured certificates of deposit. Unfortunately, it was just a scam.

Throughout the case, we gathered significant evidence showing how the firm failed to properly supervise its advisor's conduct and how it overlooked numerous and glaring red flags indicating illegal activity. While we had a strong case, we also had a problem: the brokerage firm had little money. Its audited financials painted a grim picture, and its regulatory filings showed a growing list of claimants filing complaints against the firm. Unfortunately, there are many small brokerage firms with woefully inadequate funding, and we often see this problem.

In the course of settlement discussions, the brokerage firm's lawyer conveyed a final offer of $100,000, take it or leave it. The labor union made a tough but smart business decision by agreeing to accept the $100,000 that was on the table. Not long after the settlement proceeds were paid, regulators announced that the brokerage firm was fined $1 million and going out of business.

You may be wondering how you learn about the financial condition of your broker and their firm. Remember the following points when making your selection and you'll likely sleep more peacefully at night.

NO INSURANCE, NO PROBLEM?

You can't drive without car insurance. I can't effectively represent clients without legal malpractice insurance. These requirements have been developed over time to protect the public, necessary protections for a developed society. But when it comes to our financial security, do the professionals we hire to help us have their own liability insurance? It may surprise you to discover that the professionals who manage our wealth and retirement savings are not required by the federal securities regulators to have insurance.

Some firms are self-insured, and they have sufficient resources in most circumstances to withstand large claims. Think Wells Fargo, Merrill Lynch, Morgan Stanley, and UBS, for example. If you choose to work with one of these firms, you most likely won't have to worry about their ability to pay a legal claim if you prevail.

But I mentioned before that about 3,500 brokerage firms exist in the country—names of most you have probably never heard. If you're deciding whether you should hire one of these firms, it's important that you keep reading this section.

Professional liability insurance policies are available for purchase by firms and brokers. You'll find that some firms have them. How do you know if your firm has liability insurance for claims that are covered? The answer is not so simple.

Firms are not required to disclose whether they have insurance, so you have to ask. Your broker should clearly identify the broker-dealer with whom they are affiliated and whether they have or their firm has liability insurance, including possible exclusions and policy limits. Any reputable broker with nothing to hide will be upfront and transparent. I recommend you obtain this information in writing.

However, even if a firm or broker does have liability insurance, the policies typically have enormously problematic policy exclusions. For example, they almost never cover intentional misconduct. I would say roughly half of my investment cases are categorized by the insurance company as "intentional misconduct."

I recently handled a case against a firm on behalf of a single mom who was heavily invested in inverse-leveraged exchange-traded funds (ETFs). She had lost her entire investment. We filed the case and requested a copy of the policy exclusions. Not surprisingly, leveraged ETFs were specifically excluded from coverage. Her financial advisor was facing an onslaught of legal claims that matched my client's, and there weren't enough resources to go around. Despite my client having a solid legal claim, the defendants couldn't pay her.

Nothing is worse than having your money stolen, hiring a lawyer, proving that you were wronged, and still never seeing a penny of your savings again. Let's revisit our example with Brian, the broker who was too good to be true. If you had asked him during your initial interview whether he had insurance and he responded that he did not, should you have cut him loose and continued your search? Not necessarily.

The question becomes, if you lose your $1 million because they messed up, do they have the resources to pay you back without insurance coverage? It's the million-dollar question with an answer you must know before you invest. No matter how many rules, regulations, and laws are created to protect investors, all are meaningless if an investor is unable to recover their money when these rules, regulations, and laws are violated. It's the sad truth that investors who become victims of financial misconduct can also be victims of a second abuse: the inability to collect an arbitration or court judgment issued against the financial advisor and/or firm found liable.

YOU CAN'T SQUEEZE BLOOD FROM A TURNIP

Every year, investors file meritorious cases against brokers, investment advisers, and financial firms for their misconduct and, every year, the stack of unpaid investor judgments piles up. This is an enormous problem in the United States that can be attributed to a lack of legislative action and proper industry safeguards.

Statistics released by FINRA show that in a recent five-year period, a total of $199 million in awards went unpaid, or 27 percent of cases won by investors. An investor hires an investment fraud attorney, files a case, wins the case, then never receives payment in one out of every four cases. I participate in legislative lobbying efforts and engage in discussions with regulators and policy makers to bring awareness to this issue with hopes of resolving it someday soon. Until policies change, this remains a serious risk for every investor.

So how do you mitigate this risk? You start digging.

BROKER-DEALERS AND NET CAPITAL

All FINRA broker-dealers are required to file, on an annual basis, audited financials. These filings are free and publicly available on www.sec.gov/edgar. You can ask a firm for their financials by requesting Form X-17A-5, also known as a focus report.

EDGAR is an acronym that stands for Electronic Data Gathering, Analysis, and Retrieval system. Densely packed with financial details, these documents contain the broker-dealer's net capital reporting. The higher the reported net capital, the more money the firm has in the bank. If you're considering entrusting $1 million to a firm that's probably managing tens or hundreds of millions of dollars collectively and has available capital of roughly $500,000 with no insurance, EDGAR is where you would find these unfortunate, yet helpful, facts.

The net capital of broker-dealers in this country spans a wide range. Some have hundreds of millions of dollars. Some report a measly $50,000 of net capital. You may even find that some firms report a *negative* net capital and promise the SEC that additional funds will be available soon. These reported financials are vital for your analysis of a firm's financial solvency, yet the average investor rarely takes this step. My advice: If you are considering hiring a broker who works for a smaller brokerage firm (one that is not a household name), I strongly encourage you to do the research discussed before you hand over your hard-earned money.

INVESTMENT ADVISERS AND ASSETS UNDER MANAGEMENT

The roughly 13,000 investment adviser firms in the United States (with whom approximately 100,000 investment advisers are affiliated) are not required to annually report net capital and don't have the same filing requirements as broker-dealers. Instead, they file with the SEC Form ADVs, a report containing the amount of assets under management.

Just as with broker-dealers, the assets under management vary widely among investment adviser firms. Some manage more than $30 billion, while smaller firms manage less than

$50 million. These are undoubtedly large numbers, but it's important to remember that this is the summation of client money managed, not the available funds of the investment adviser or the firm. This number can, however, indicate the financial well-being of the firm. A firm that manages $30 billion is going to make a great deal more in fees than one that manages $50 million. Form ADVs are submitted annually and found at www.advisorinfo.sec.gov.

Now that you understand the differences between brokers and investment advisers, and have vital information for choosing the *type* of advisor to hire, let's discuss how to check *whom* you are hiring.

CAN I SEE YOUR LICENSE AND REGISTRATION?

Would you knowingly work with brokers or investment advisers who have been the subject of dozens of customer lawsuits as a result of their misconduct? How about someone fired for failing to follow firm policies? Would you entrust your life savings to someone who doesn't have a securities license? How about someone convicted of theft?

Believe it or not, the investment industry is littered with bad apples. But there's good news. At your fingertips, you have a quick and easy way to find out whom you're really working with.

From the comfort of your living room couch, you can complete a free background check on any broker or advisor by visiting www.BrokerCheck.finra.org.[4] Simply enter your prospective broker or advisor's name and pull up the report that lists investor need-to-know items:

- The licenses they hold and the states where they are registered to sell securities or provide investment advice.
- Prior customer complaints, the basis of the complaint, and whether they are resolved.
- Terminations.
- Regulatory actions and investigations.
- Criminal charges.
- Financial disclosures, such as bankruptcy filings, liens, or outstanding judgments.
- Whether they have disclosed involvement in any outside businesses separate from their work as a broker or advisor.

It's important to understand that this public resource is not 100 percent accurate. Brokers are able, in particular circumstances, to erase reportable events in a process known as "expungement." When a broker is able to have prior customer complaints expunged, or erased, from their public record, prospective customers will no longer have access to that information when reviewing the broker's public report. Ultimately, there's no way to know for sure that the infor-

---

4   While the starting page for searching brokers and investment advisers is the same, if you select someone who is an investment adviser only, you will be directed to the SEC's report after selecting the advisor. Luckily, you don't need to know in advance whether the person is a broker or an investment adviser because BrokerCheck will tell you.

mation in the BrokerCheck report is complete, but it's far better to know some information than nothing at all.

You can also refine your search by entering extra details, such as the firm name, city, state, or zip code. With hundreds of thousands of brokers and investment advisers working in the United States, it's likely that a single name query will turn up multiple results. Searching for "William Smith," for instance, results in 309 entries. The more specific information you have about your broker, the easier your search.

Another valuable resource you have is your state securities administrator. Their information is available at www.nasaa.org/contact-your-regulator/.

What happens if you search for prospective financial professionals, and they don't appear on BrokerCheck or the SEC website? Run away. Don't walk. This means they are not licensed, which means you should not give them any money. One of the biggest problems in the investment world is the existence of unlicensed fraudsters promoting the sale of unregistered securities. We field an overwhelming number of phone calls from people who lost money in investment scams working with random, unlicensed people they thought were trustworthy. It's heartbreaking to tell victims that nothing can be done to recover their lost money. These scammers have no licenses and no financial institutions to which they are affiliated and, therefore, no feasible way to pursue the recovery of the losses on behalf of the investor.

The majority of financial advisors who are properly licensed and registered have no disclosures on their reports, although a small percentage[5] have many. In my experience, investors working with brokers who have an alarming number of disclosures have no idea of either the disclosures or the reports that are available to them. Brokerage firms certainly don't openly offer this information at the beginning of a relationship. You're never going to hear, "Hey, we've been sued 27 times because of this broker. Are you sure you want to work with him?" It's up to you to do your research and decide whether you're willing to take a chance.

Various studies have analyzed broker recidivism and whether past customer complaints and disciplinary events predict if brokers will become repeat offenders. A 2016 study found that the rate of recidivism in the first year after a misconduct disclosure is nearly 20 times the average for misconduct. It remains five times above average five years after a misconduct disclosure. My experience supports these conclusions. If brokers or investment advisers con one client, they will probably do it again given the opportunity.

---

5   I wish I could be more specific here, but the system is not transparent. Various attempts have been made to evaluate disclosures and investor harm relative to the total number of brokers and investment advisers, but FINRA doesn't make BrokerCheck data available in bulk to all those interested in analyzing the data. If BrokerCheck's information were truly publicly available, researchers, third-party vendors, ratings companies, and news outlets could rank brokerage firms on the risk of fraud.

I am personally lobbying regulators to improve one particular inadequacy with BrokerCheck to better serve the investing public. Currently, regulators record customer complaints and regulatory matters at the broker level. Investors can only look up data at the broker level and not at the firm level. FINRA presents the data in a way that makes it impossible for investors to see an accurate picture of firm-level misconduct.

With a typical search, an investor may look up a broker with the name of Smith and see his work history and complaints. But what about the other brokers at his firm? What is the culture of the firm that trains and supervises him? By connecting the brokers' history with the culture of the firms who employ them, the investing public can gain a more complete picture of who they are trusting with their life savings. FINRA must report the BrokerCheck date cumulatively and at the firm level. As the current president of PIABA, I am working hard to make this happen.

The name of one particularly bad broker was spoken in our firm's hallways for years. His name was Terry, and he amassed 73 customer complaints as a broker the majority of which were handled by my law firm. In most professions, it takes only a few instances of misconduct for an employee to be shown the door. In Terry's case, and as reported in the public records, it cost his large brokerage firm $13 million in settlements before he was finally fired. Despite the complaints and a regulatory investigation, Terry was permitted to stay with the firm and continued, for years, to manage and invest his clients' life savings. His BrokerCheck report reflecting his numerous misconduct disclosures remains the thickest and worst report I've come across.

His clients, of course, had no idea who Terry really was. When he was finally fired, he was picked up by a much smaller broker-dealer and took many of his unsuspecting clients with him. There, he continued on his deceptive path and sold thirty-nine of his clients into a Ponzi scheme, losing more than $7 million. Finally, after years of misconduct, Terry was barred from the securities industry and sentenced to 57 months in prison.

Had Terry's clients known about his past misconduct, they most likely would never have agreed to give him the funds for the Ponzi scheme. But not one client had reviewed his BrokerCheck report. The firm certainly didn't warn their customers, even after Terry was fired. A quick review of BrokerCheck would have likely saved many investors heartache, uncertainty, and a lengthy legal battle to recover their money.

It's more likely that brokers with personal financial problems of their own will try to create financial issues for others by lying, cheating, or stealing their way to personal gain.

Brian from our earlier example sold inappropriate high-commission products in a desperate attempt to dig himself out of crushing debt. A peek into Brian's BrokerCheck report would have revealed numerous unpaid debts. Do you really want someone who struggles with managing their own money managing yours? It's the supervisors' job at the firm to carefully watch their broker or advisor, but you can do some homework, as well. A simple calendar reminder will let you know when it's time to check up on your broker on an annual basis. If your search returns a disclosure, discuss it with the supervisor and reevaluate your relationship. Knowledge, after all, is power.

Next, in Part 2, we'll explore just how deep dishonesty can run in the financial industry and how, to some, greed is everything.

Most Financial Advisors Don't Lie, Cheat, or Steal—but Some Do

Picking the right person and firm to trust with your life savings is only half the battle. It's easy to be lulled into a sense of security over time. Maybe you've worked with financial advisors for so long that they feel like family—so much so that even the suggestion that they're not entirely straight-laced elicits shock and outrage.

This is exactly where dishonest financial advisors want you to be. Without vigilance and just a hint of skepticism, you can become an easy target for manipulation and misconduct.

In Part 2, we'll explore the misconduct I most frequently see in the financial industry, a few of the craziest cases I've handled over the past 20 years as an investment fraud lawyer, and how you can tell if something isn't right with your investment.

CHAPTER 3

———

Greed: The Dark Side of the American Dream

The 1987 movie *Wall Street* was my first foray into the world of stockbrokers. The economy of the 1980s, of course, was the pinnacle of speculative trading, before computers were widely used. In those days, broker phone banks on Long Island were the epicenters of legendary sales. While brokers' sales strategies have evolved, the same problems that plagued the industry in the 1980s still plague it today. If brokers want to lie, cheat, or steal, they will often find a way.

In this chapter, we'll talk about the real fraudsters of the investing world—the shady brokers and investment advisers who cast a dark shadow on the industry. They find creative ways to take your money, hoping they get away with it. Some of their strategies are inventive; others are shockingly manipulative. No matter how they do it, fraudsters always leave their victims wondering, "How did this happen?"

Financial criminals don't look like criminals. They often look like the upstanding professionals that they should be. People employed by some of the country's leading financial firms commit fraud all the time, often right under the noses of their supervisors.

Occasionally, investors face the consequences of their broker's innocent or lazy mistake. Maybe their broker incorrectly enters a transaction order or overlooks a box while completing paperwork. Lawsuits and arbitration cases in these instances are few and far between. What I typically deal with on a daily basis is the result of unchecked, pervasive greed.

It seems like we want more of everything as a society. Generally, seeking prosperity and growth is a good thing. This drive fuels innovation and development. We become better people and live better as a whole—generally.

But for an ample minority, wanting more becomes a greed-laden pursuit of wealth in an audacious and blatantly insensitive display of disregard for others. It's this psychological phenomenon that has separated individual investors from their hard-earned dollars throughout the last century.

During the early days of my career, I frequently asked myself an important question: Why? Why would anyone take such a huge risk and manipulate their clients? I imagine a normal-looking man shaving his face in the morning and peering into the mirror, thinking to himself, *I wonder if today is the day the Feds will raid my office.*

Investment fraud is always uncovered at some point. Schemes eventually unravel, lies and manipulation are discovered, and the broker faces public embarrassment, expulsion, restitution, and sometimes jail time. Back then, I could not fathom why anyone would risk it all, no matter how much money was at stake.

The last 20 years have shown me plenty of society's worst humans. It's become clear that chasing money, to the detriment of everything else in a fraudster's life, becomes addicting for these people. Plenty has been written by prominent psychologists about greed as an addiction. For that dopamine kick, a greed addict must acquire "bigger" and "better"—the next fancy car, yacht, estate, or penthouse. They wind up in a cycle of taking merciless advantage of those around them. Maybe they see the end result, but they cannot stop. At some point, they cross the line and can't—or won't—look back.

In some cases, deceptive financial advisors are caught in the act at the start of their bad behavior. Perhaps they haven't committed fraud, but they've chosen to sell wildly inappropriate investments to their clients for no other reason than to generate more money for themselves. It might be holding back vital information the client needs to make an informed choice, or it could be flat out lying to clients just to make a sale.

I don't question bad brokers' motives anymore. I've seen it all, and brokers or investment advisers can take advantage of you in almost limitless ways. Let's explore some of the most pervasive approaches I've seen representing victims of investment fraud over the past 20 years.

THE FINANCIAL EXPLOITATION OF SENIORS

The famous bank robber of the early 1900s, Willie Sutton, was once asked why he robbed banks. His response? "Because that's where the money is."

Our senior clients are the vulnerable ones. Currently, Americans 65 and older comprise the segment of population with a projected growth of 86 million by 2050, according to the Pew Research Group. Senior financial exploitation is quickly becoming the most serious consumer threat of our lifetime. In 2018, the SEC reported that elder financial exploitation has risen to 6.6 percent of the senior population, with figures likely underreported.[6] In fact, for every documented case of

6   www.sec.gov/files/elder-financial-exploitation.pdf

elder financial exploitation, 44 were unreported, according to a study completed by the state of New York in 2016.[7]

Seniors are easier targets, and for a good reason: they typically have worked their entire lives creating a nest egg for themselves and their families. Fraudsters wouldn't waste their time trying to pry money out of most 30-year-olds because this age group doesn't have a lot of money. Seniors are also sometimes isolated, living alone and potentially with cognitive decline. Many just aren't as sharp as they once were, and they're often dependent on others.

The horrible things people do to vulnerable seniors are deeply distressing. I once had a client whose own daughter kept him drugged so that he was too disoriented to notice she was draining his investment accounts with a fraudulent power of attorney. When the investment account was locked because of suspicious activity, she took him into a branch office to verify his identity. The advisor was so concerned about this man's state that he called Adult Protective Services. Still, the account was unlocked, and the daughter was able to finish draining it.

This particular situation presented a solid case against the broker-dealer. Financial institutions play a key role in detecting and preventing elder financial exploitation. If they fail in

---

7   https://ocfs.ny.gov/main/reports/Cost%20of%20Financial%20Exploitation%20Study%20
FINAL%20May%202016.pdf

their duty to safeguard their clients' assets and the customer is harmed as a result, the firm can be held responsible for losses. In this case with many red flags, the firm agreed the client was in trouble. Still, they allowed the activity to continue, even after contacting authorities.

Sometimes, clients' advance directives are altered by their financial advisors to benefit the financial advisors. I have represented many clients who were coerced into making their financial advisors the beneficiaries or executors of their estates. One broker added a provision to my client's will stating that the broker's daughter would receive substantial sums. I've seen financial advisors sell seniors prohibitively expensive life insurance policies and then make themselves the beneficiary of the policies.

The misconduct can be more subtle and manifest simply as selling seniors inappropriate investments. One of my clients was sold a non-traded real estate investment trust[8] while she was recovering in the hospital from a stroke. The broker argued that he explained all the risks associated with the investment to her and that she fully understood what was happening. I had to present her medical records to show how that would have been impossible.

The compliance and supervisory personnel at financial insti-

---

8   An incredibly expensive, risky, illiquid investment that a senior (or any retail investor) has no business buying, in my view.

tutions are an important line of defense in combating senior exploitation. Firms are required to consider their customers' ages when supervising their accounts.

It's important to be on the lookout for potential indicators of senior financial exploitation:

- Erratic or unusual banking transactions, or changes in banking patterns.
- An inexplicable change in investment objectives or risk tolerance.
- Making investments that don't match the customer's investment objectives or risk tolerance.
- Uncharacteristic withdrawals or attempts to wire large sums of money.
- Nonpayment for services.
- Closing of CDs or accounts without regard to penalties.
- A caregiver or other individual showing excessive interest in a seniors' finances or assets, not allowing them to speak for themselves or seem reluctant to leave their side during conversations.
- The financial institution is unable to speak directly with the elders, despite repeated attempts to contact them.

Who better to help protect these vulnerable seniors than professionals at the financial institutions who are trained to identify potential warning signs?

An important way senior investors help protect themselves is by adding a "trusted contact person" to their investment account. A trusted contact person lacks authority to authorize the purchase or sale of securities in an account but is authorized as a contact person when a brokerage firm identifies potentially suspicious activity in an account or has had difficulty contacting the account owner. Every brokerage firm has a form you can complete and sign to add a trusted contact person to your account. I encourage everyone, but especially senior investors, to take this simple step.

A few years ago, a stockbroker contacted me about a theft from his mother-in-law's investment accounts that were held by a different brokerage firm. As someone who had worked in the securities business for many years, he was appalled at what the other brokerage firm allowed to transpire in these accounts.

The story of Kathleen, his mother-in-law, is heartbreaking. In the months following her husband's death, she fell prey to a person posing as a prospective love interest on an online dating site for seniors. Kathleen believed that this person, whose real identity is unknown to this day, was going to take care of her, and she started transferring money to him with the belief that she was investing in her soon-to-be new husband's business. She fell in love and believed she had found someone who would provide her with the emotional support and security she felt she desperately needed since her husband's death. Eventually, under duress and intimidation, Kathleen continued to send money for what she believed her future husband was using to finish a business project in Malaysia. Unfortunately, this was an elaborate scam.

The evidence showed that Kathleen's investment accounts depleted rapidly over a three-month timeframe. About six months after her husband's death, Kathleen's investment accounts were valued at approximately $355,000. This included an individual account with a balance of about $270,000 and an IRA with a balance of about $85,000. Under the brokerage firm's watch, these accounts started rapidly draining. Remarkably, in three months' time, the individual account was worth $107.38 and the IRA was worth just $0.11.

As we worked the case, we learned that shortly before the withdrawals from Kathleen's accounts, her financial advisor had attended a firm-sponsored training about senior financial abuse. The training materials identified several specific red flags for financial advisors, including when an investor loses a family member and assumes responsibility for finances after the death of a spouse, and when financial advisors notice unusual transactions or request large sums of money. Each one of these red flags was staring Kathleen's financial advisor square in the face as her accounts were being drained. Why didn't he do anything to stop it?

But as sometimes happens in my line of work, I also learned

some facts that were unhelpful to my client's case. As it turned out, when the withdrawals began, Kathleen's advisor did, in fact, ask her about the transactions. She told him she needed the money for a remodeling project, which, of course, was not true. As Kathleen's lawyer, I understood that when she made this statement to her advisor, she didn't want to reveal her newfound love interest. Even so, her apparent lack of candor didn't help her argument that the brokerage firm failed to reasonably inquire about the withdrawals. Furthermore, the brokerage firm argued that besides Kathleen, there was no trusted contact person or anyone else authorized to contact regarding Kathleen's accounts.

In the end, we were able to negotiate a nice settlement for Kathleen. But her entire situation may have been avoided if she had identified a trusted contact person on her investment accounts.

IT'S IN THE DETAILS

The trick of manipulation is in the presentation. Fraudsters are adept at forming deep personal bonds with their clients then exploiting the trust they've built over time. I had a case a few years ago in the Midwest with a husband and wife, Mike and Diana, who were taken advantage of by a young financial advisor, Ben, who developed a deep personal relationship with them. Mike and Diana always loved kids but never had children of their own. Over time, Ben became the son they'd never had. He spoke with Mike and Diana frequently but rarely about their investments. They would spend long periods of time talking about Ben's personal life, keeping up-to-date with his career, young family, and anything new. The couple even attended birthday parties for Ben's children. And when his marriage hit some rough patches, Mike and Diana were there to provide solace and counsel.

But behind all of these deeply personal interactions, Ben was ripping off Mike and Diana. They became the victims of Ben's lengthy scheme with investments called, "unit investment trusts" (UITs). UITs are similar to mutual funds and intended as long-term investments, but Ben frequently purchased and held UITs in Mike's and Diana's accounts for only a few months at a time before selling and purchasing different UITs, generating a commission on each purchase and sale. Throughout seven years of investment, Ben generated nearly $300,000 in commissions that were concealed from the couple because the commission, or "load," was built into the purchase price of the product, as is common with UITs and mutual funds. Ben was then paid a separate selling concession directly from the UIT or mutual fund company. This information was buried deep in the product's more-than-100-page prospectus, not disclosed in trade confirmations or account statements.

Seven years after first meeting Ben, Mike and Diana began to wonder why they hadn't seen growth in their accounts.

After their CPA reviewed their accounts, he referred them to my law firm. Mike and Diana were stunned to learn that someone they'd treated as their son ripped them off for seven years. Essentially, all the gains and capital appreciation that should have accrued in their accounts became Ben's commissions. The accounts stayed flat while Ben was paid roughly $40,000 per year from his trades with the couple's money.

No matter how much you think you can trust your advisor, I always recommend that you have another trusted person, such as a family member, CPA, an attorney, or unbiased friend review your financial statements periodically to make sure you're not being taken advantage of the way that Mike and Diana were.

AFFINITY FRAUD

For deceptive brokers, sometimes the goal is not only to find the right victim and befriend them but also to work their way into the investor's trusted circle. Nothing works better for fraudsters than to share—or pretend to share—the same values with their victims.

"Affinity fraud" is the exploitation of the trust and friendships shared amongst a group of people. This tight-knit structure makes it tough for outsiders to learn about any fraud occurring within. You'll find affinity fraud in professional groups, religious groups, and ethnic communities.

I once represented a group of 75 families from California who were all of Fijian descent. One deceitful broker, Raj, was referred from family to family in this community like a chain reaction until he was managing everyone's investments. In their eyes, he was a prominent and successful financial expert.

However, Raj persuaded 190 members of the Fijian community to invest in a fraud that grossed approximately $20 million. He told investors that he was using their money for what is known as "hard-money lending," and that returns were guaranteed. In reality, he used the money for gambling, personal expenses, and to pay other investors their "guaranteed" returns so he could keep his scheme going. He was sentenced to 15 years in prison. We recovered money for the victims in a case against the brokerage firm with which he was affiliated.

The ethnic community connection is ripe for affinity fraud, as is the religious community connection. I represented several families whose financial advisor was also a pastor in their church. After they became clients, he met with them and told them that his daughter had a religious prophecy that the dollar was ready to collapse imminently. The only way to protect themselves, he said, would be to invest everything into a single hard-currency fund.

I have no way to explain the pastor/advisor's motivation other than to think that he must have truly believed his daughter's prophecy. I've seen the "world is ending" mentality spur brokers into doing bizarre things with their clients' portfolios before. As a general rule, if a broker touts an apocalyptic-type event on the horizon and suggests you liquidate entirely out of the market (buy all gold, for example), I suggest you find a new broker!

The religious aspect of this man's advice coupled with his pastoral role had his clients rushing to accept his recommendation. They lost a ton of money. Although it took them a very long time to find fault with his advice, eventually they realized that as a financial advisor, he had an obligation to avoid mixing his roles and responsibilities.

In another example of affinity fraud in religion, a stockbroker solicited his clients to invest in a small local television station that provided religious programming. This small outfit, the sales pitch went, was about to become a nationally branded Christian cable network. The stockbroker had spent years establishing a client base of folks he met at local churches, bible meetings, and other religious functions. He spoke openly about his faith, and his clients believed he was a person they could trust. This included my client, Robert, an active churchgoer who had known the broker for many years and was unwittingly a ripe target for his misconduct.

As it turned out, unbeknownst to his customers, the broker had fallen on hard times and faced a large stack of unpaid tax bills. Desperately in need of money, he entered into an informal and illegal business relationship with the owner of the local Christian television station. The idea was that the broker would recommend to his customers an investment of "preferred shares" issued by the station, producing a handsome payment for the broker. By law, stockbrokers cannot sell any investments that are not approved by their supervising brokerage firm. The purpose behind such prohibition is straightforward: it's critical that brokerage firms conduct extensive due diligence on any investment before the firm allows its brokers to sell the investment to its clients.

In this case, the broker's firm had not approved the sale of the preferred shares. In fact, the firm claimed that it was unaware that the broker was selling these investments to his clients and that it only became aware of his misconduct after my firm filed claims on Robert's behalf. We alleged, among other things, that the brokerage firm failed to supervise its broker. Robert, of course, was unaware that his broker was selling an unapproved investment. In fact, he was shocked when he learned that he had been duped. Even so, if Robert had been aware of affinity fraud, he may have been more skeptical about the investment he sold.

Ideally, Robert could have protected himself if he had asked his broker a few key questions at the outset:

- Have these investments been approved by your brokerage firm? If so, please provide a copy of the written approval.

- What sort of due diligence did your firm conduct on these investments?
- How much are you paid to sell these investments? What are your commissions from this investment?

Financial advisors can manipulate investors in a variety of ways, with a variety of tools at their disposal. In the next chapter, we'll talk about all the tools fraudsters use in their schemes—tools that are undeniably impressive *and* often criminal.

CHAPTER 4

———

Tools of the (Criminal) Trade

It's important that you can trust your financial advisor. Despite the warnings and tales of caution I've shared, you can trust the majority of those with whom you come in contact. You don't have to live in a state of constant paranoia, but common sense, proactive diligence, and mild skepticism can save you a lot of future pain. Think of it in the words of Ronald Reagan: "Trust, but verify."

IS IT THE REAL DEAL?

In the world of investment, it's easy to find yourself in a "too much of a good thing" situation when it comes to trust. When you end up with a bad apple for a financial advisor, common sense can only help you so much.

Fraudulent account statements, faxes, emails, hand-delivered notices, and misleading promotional materials have all been used as tools of deception in cases I've handled. Twenty years ago, it was nearly impossible to find convincing fake account statements. With advancements in computer programming and inexpensive editing software, however, it's easy to create false documents that look impressively official.

I've seen a multitude of ways a broker can convince a client to rely on fabricated numbers. First and foremost, the broker has to keep the client from actually receiving the authentic account statements.

When you open an investment account, institutions cram "paperless" options down your throat. Paperless delivery is now commonplace, primarily because firms don't want the expense of mailing paper statements or trade confirmations to you.

To have the option of retrieving statements electronically, you first have to establish online access. A large percentage of my clients never set this up because they simply don't know how. What may seem even more surprising is that a large percentage of clients without online access also don't spend a lot of time reading their paper statements. After all, they believe they don't need to; their financial advisor provides them with all the information they need.

If you're currently enrolled in online financial statements, do you actually take the time to click on the monthly link that logs you into your account? Do you, without fail, make the extra effort to ensure your account is running smoothly and according to the plan designed and implemented by your financial advisor? There are log-in credentials to remember, passwords to change every two months, and 10 steps of security to pass when you log in from a new device. It's not that online banking is hard; it's just easier to pass on your monthly statement email and rely on your financial advisor for updates and important information.

Gianni and Clara were an elderly immigrant couple from Greece and had worked with a large national brokerage firm for 15 years when I first met them. Both were retired doctors. They were smart, educated people who trusted their broker completely. He visited them once every quarter with an account summary—a visit the couple always looked forward to. According to these summaries, things were going quite well.

One Christmas, their adult son visited from out of town. He asked his parents questions about their investments, and their answers concerned him. Not only were they unable to tell him the investments in their portfolio, they never received trade confirmations because their broker visited several times a year to update them directly. Their son asked to see an account statement; he had his own accounts with the same firm and knew that his parents' statements would give him all the missing information he needed. One look at them and he realized that something was very wrong: not all of the account numbers matched and the statements didn't look like other statements he had seen in the past.

A few phone calls later with the broker's supervisor, Gianni and Clara discovered that the $3 million of investments they thought were in their portfolio had actually been wiped out when their broker invested their money in high-risk investments against their wishes. To keep up the facade so his clients wouldn't learn of the losses, the broker created a different set of statements himself.

You may be thinking that he was probably a rookie, or possibly worked at a small branch of the firm. How could anyone with industry experience pull such a risky stunt? This broker was, in fact, the vice president of a large branch office of a huge national brokerage firm. After this case, he would never work in the investment business again. This particular broker may have been trying to cover up an enormous error, but some brokers use the fraudulent tactic of creating fake client materials as a strategy to make millions.

One such schemer in Pennsylvania was named Susan. She ran a longstanding Ponzi scheme out of her small office in Pittsburgh, generating phony account statements for years. Unlike Gianni's and Clara's statements, these statements looked like the real deal and could have fooled even a trained eye. Susan had gone so far as to hire an art student from a local technical college to recreate statements that looked exactly like those from her supervising brokerage firm. Everything on the statements looked real: the account numbers and balances, the securities holdings, and the office address.

I was initially contacted by one of Susan's victims on a sunny Saturday afternoon during Memorial Day weekend. Gary was a salesman in his fifties who had more than $2 million invested with Susan—at least he thought he had $2 million, until the FBI informed him that Susan had used his money for her own interests. Gary and several other individuals and families hired my firm to bring claims against Susan's supervising brokerage firm in an effort to recover their life savings.

When fake account statements like Susan's are difficult to separate from the real ones, how do you know something is wrong? You've done everything we've discussed so far to ensure your money is safe: you've researched your broker, checked his/her registrations, checked on the affiliated firm, and reviewed your statements regularly. The truth is, no matter how much you trust your broker, you should always periodically call their supervising brokerage firm and confirm your account balance and related information.

This is how Susan's elaborate scheme unraveled. One of her customers called the home office of her firm requesting account information, and the firm had no record of the customer. The inquiry tipped off the firm about potential wrongdoing, and they quickly dispatched compliance investigators to Susan's single-person office.

We filed a case against this brokerage firm alleging that it failed to adequately supervise the broker, and we learned that the brokerage firm's emergency visit to Susan's office was remarkably only the second time in four years that anyone from the compliance department had bothered to visit Susan's office. Within minutes of arriving, the firm's investigators uncovered substantial evidence of fraud: phony statements, emails, letters, and a variety of electronic records. Every false document was created and maintained onsite, at Susan's office. She made no effort to conceal her misconduct from her supervising brokerage firm's compliance department. When Susan was confronted by the firm's investigators, she immediately admitted that she had been defrauding customers for years. She was arrested on federal criminal charges and eventually sentenced to prison. As for our clients? We negotiated significant settlements with Susan's brokerage firm that resulted in a substantial recovery of their losses.

You can learn multiple lessons from Susan's story. Not only should you sign up for online statements and confirm your account activity with your brokerage firm, but you should also never write a check to an entity other than the brokerage firm or the clearing firm that maintains custody of the money.

Only in rare circumstances involving annuities and private placements will investors ever be required to write a check payable to anyone else. In fact, the fine print of many brokerage firm account agreements specifically informs customers to *only* write checks payable to them. Never write a check or wire money directly to your financial advisor individually or to any entity that he/she owns.

Susan was able to get her hands on her clients' money because she told them to write checks payable to "SL Investments" and other fallacious entities. She then deposited these checks into bank accounts she had established in the names of these fake companies. Her customers believed that SL Investments was a fund held by the brokerage firm. Based on the phony account statements, customers thought their funds were being deposited at the brokerage firm and used to purchase legitimate securities, including corporate bonds issued by companies like General Electric, The Hershey Company, McDonald's Corporation, and Ford Motor Company.

So what did Susan do with all the money? She used her clients' retirements to fuel her gambling habit. To her victims, it was like pouring salt in a wound.

SPOTTING A FAKE

How do you ensure that you're reviewing a real account statement? Whether by mail or email, make sure it comes from the one undeniably legitimate source: the custodian of your account. Brokerage firms and custodial firms like Schwab, Pershing, Ameritrade, and Fidelity, among many others, have a legal obligation to send account statements. Individual financial advisors might send performance reports, account analyses, or other account-related documents, but they should *not* send you your monthly account statements or portfolio performance documents directly.

We had a case in Arizona where the broker and his client, Steve, shared a great love of baseball and a particular team. Despite not having a personal relationship that predated their professional relationship, they spoke on the phone almost every day for several years. They mostly talked about baseball—stats, games, recruiting—but every time Steve asked how "their" account was that day, the broker cheerfully reported the market's activity and the account's worth, down to the penny. Steve relied entirely on the figures he received from his broker. He never set up access to an online account because he felt he didn't need to. Why would he? He spoke to his broker nearly every day.

One day, Steve received a call from his broker's supervisor letting him know that the broker had been terminated from the firm. Steve, concerned, asked about his investment account. He nearly had a heart attack when the supervisor told him it was valued at roughly $250,000 when just 24 hours prior his broker reported its worth at $635,000.

Steve wasn't the only victim. Several investors suffered the same fate, and the broker was fired when he was ultimately caught. This is the world we now live in, where some people don't think twice about leveraging a human connection for personal gain. Recognizing when someone is using your friendship to rip you off is a difficult feat. This is why it's important that you take every step reasonably possible to ensure that you're working with an ethical broker who tells you the truth.

DON'T PICK UP THE PHONE

Remember the days when Wall Street's minions earned most of their business by cold-calling strangers all over the country from the comfort of their high-rise offices? These young and hungry brokers with slicked-back Gordon Gekko hair didn't know much about the market. Their job was to prospect for investors all day, every day. They were trained how to ruthlessly and persistently sell by using various scripts handed to them by their bosses. Branch managers kept charts of brokers' accounts and asset growth; they didn't want their brokers to know their clients, only to hit quotas. Cold-calling, the managers surmised, would get them there.

This relentless pursuit was the way of the world through the 1990s when people had landlines and picked up their phones when they rang. As the age of the landline passed in the following decade, so, too, did phone books. People grew leery of answering phone calls from strangers, especially on their cell phones. Now, modern phones allow us to see our callers; in the past, you had to pick up the phone to learn whether it was your spouse or a salesman.

These changes forced brokerage firms to adapt. They couldn't peddle investments the same way they used to. Investors demanded relationships with their financial advisors, wanting to now meet with them face-to-face and engage with them for holistic wealth management advice rather than just hot stock tips.

When I say brokerage firms have adapted since the age of the cold call, I'm referring to *most* brokerage firms. I still receive calls from investors who were cold-called and suffered greatly as a result. The only brokers still selling investments to strangers over the phone, in my experience, are the shady ones.

I once met a random broker at a restaurant who, after a few drinks, confessed that he somehow obtained a nationwide personal contact list for owners of gas stations. He would cold call these station owners and convince them that he was affiliated with a coalition of gas station owners and was familiar with their industry. In reality, he knew nothing of gas stations or the ins-and-outs of these owners' businesses. This approach, however, was a good way to get them to trust him.

The true danger of the cold call is that, with a phone number and a brief background check, anyone anywhere in the world can manipulate you. One of my clients was a third-generation corn farmer from Minnesota named Clark. He owned 1,000 acres of prime farming land that had been passed down through his family. One day, he hoped to pass this land on to his sons.

Clark was a typical farmer: rich in assets and poor in cash. He sold his corn to cover the costs of farming every year. The little that was left went back into the farm for new machinery, seeds, and fertilizer. Investing in the stock market was the last thing on Clark's mind, something he had never done a day in his life.

Grand Securities was a broker-dealer in New York City. It was small in size but well known throughout the industry, albeit not positively. They had a bad reputation for employing the worst of the worst brokers: people whose records were so bad that no reputable firm would hire them. That didn't matter to Grand Securities. They hired bad brokers anyway and put them to work cold-calling anyone in the country who still had a landline.

One of their brokers in particular frequently targeted midwestern farmers like Clark. The broker knew that it wasn't likely Clark would have investment cash, but he may have enough collateral to take out enormous loans. One day, Clark received a call from the Grand Securities broker. When Clark told him that he had no money to invest, the broker responded with, "No problem. Take a loan from your bank, and I promise you that my trading strategy will make you immensely more than what you'll pay in interest on the loan." Not understanding the tremendous risk involved, Clark went to the bank and took out a loan for $1 million.

The broker didn't even try to hide his misconduct. Clark's account was over-traded so badly it seemed the broker didn't care about being caught. Maybe he had gotten away with it so many times in the past that he believed the regulators would never catch up to him.[9] While Clark lost his entire $1 million, the broker earned nearly $500,000 in commissions from the trades.

We brought this case against Grand Securities for allowing this to happen, and we won. All the money went to the bank to pay off Clark's massive loan, and he returned to life as he knew it before he met the broker.

Another remarkable cold-calling story involved Edward. At the time he contacted my firm, Edward was in his early seventies and near the end of a long career as a successful businessman. He had a net worth that exceeded $20 mil-

---

9   Because this case was so egregious, I occasionally look up this broker on BrokerCheck to see if he's finally been sanctioned by regulators. As of publication, this broker is still working in the industry. Not a single state or federal regulator has investigated him, and he still manages investors' money.

lion and accounts with various brokerage firms, banks, and insurance companies.

Edward contacted my firm because he'd received a letter from FINRA informing him that it was investigating one of his brokers and wanted to ask Edward some questions about his dealings with the broker. The investment account at issue was not a particularly important account to Edward, but it did begin with a cold call. He had deposited about $182,000 into the account, a small amount of money to Edward. He knew the account performed poorly, but he chalked it up to market losses and was willing to look past it because he was not a litigious person. But the letter from FINRA piqued Edward's curiosity, and he called me to see if he had any legal options.

The first thing I did for Edward was look up the broker's regulatory history on FINRA's BrokerCheck website. It was atrocious. While the broker was no longer registered with a security firm, he'd worked for 12 different brokerage firms over a 19-year span. During this time, he was the subject of at least nine other customer complaints, several of which resulted in combined settlements in excess of $1.1 million. He was also the subject of numerous tax liens totaling more than $250,000. In addition to everything else, several customer complaints were still pending that involved allegations of unauthorized trading and churning.

I informed Edward that, based on the broker's history, it

made sense for him to put together a list of all of his broker-age account statements so we could see if he had a case for excessive trading. As I explained to Edward, simply because he was a millionaire didn't give his broker a license to rip him off.

Edward's account statements proved exactly what I expected: his broker had been churning the account, making excessive trades solely for the purpose of generating high commissions that made him rich at his client's expense.

To prove churning, we have to demonstrate that the broker took control of the account and engaged in excessive trading. This involves complicated analyses that can't be done on the back of an envelope. One relatively straightforward measure involves looking at the annualized turnover rate in an account; that is, the rate at which investments are swapped out and replaced by other investments on an annual basis. Under the law, an annualized turnover rate in an investment account of six or higher is generally considered conclusive proof of excessive trading. In Edward's case, the annual turn-over rate was 48.63, or more than *eight times* the threshold of what is considered conclusively excessive.

Another measure we examined in Edward's case was the annual cost/equity ratio for the account, which is the per-centage of return necessary to pay the costs of trading. The number we calculated for Edward's account was staggering at 118.35 percent. In other words, to justify the volume of trading in Edward's account, his broker needed to earn an utterly impossible annual return of more than 118 percent.

Altogether, of the $182,000 that Edward deposited into the account, more than $153,000 went to pay commissions and markups charged by the brokerage firm. Prior to contacting my firm, Edward chalked up his losses to a bad market. The truth was that the money he lost was lining the brokerage firm's pockets.

As Edward's case developed, the brokerage firm tried to defend itself by pointing to a few so-called "happiness letters" it had sent to Edward. Brokerage firms are required to monitor investment accounts to help protect customers against harmful activity like the churning that occurred in Edward's account. But when possible improper activity is flagged, all too often a firm's first step is to insulate itself from legal responsibility. They do this by sending a "happiness letter" to the customer, a letter designed to gain investor acknowledgment that they're satisfied with the account even though the firm knows something suspicious has occurred. The happiness letter sent to Edward was received two weeks after the account was opened, a month before the churning began. The firm sent another happiness letter to Edward two years later, long after his account was decimated by markups and commissions.

The brokerage firm in Edward's case was represented by

one of Wall Street's top brokerage defense law firms. We ultimately agreed to mediate the case. At mediation, the defense lawyer huffed and puffed about how the happiness letters absolved his client of any responsibility. But I believe he recognized that the letters were a transparent attempt at CYA, covering their a**es. After a long battle, the brokerage firm agreed to pay Edward nearly all the money he lost.

The lesson here? Treat happiness letters sent from your brokerage firm as a red flag that something is wrong. Take immediate steps to protect your rights as an investor.

Happiness letters typically come from a branch manager or compliance officer, not your individual broker or financial advisor. They begin with a seemingly bland note of thanks for being a valued customer with language designed to lull you into thinking that nothing is wrong. Happiness letters typically mention the results of a periodic, routine review of the activity in your account. From there, you'll read a lot of industry jargon that is confusing to most customers *and* to those working in the securities industry. The letter typically concludes with another note of thanks and may request that you kindly sign and return the letter to the brokerage firm.

Most investors make the mistake of throwing these letters away after reading them, or, even worse, signing and mailing them back to the firm even though they may be confused or even unaware of the activity in their accounts. Brokerage firms will try to use a signed and returned happiness letter to their advantage when a dispute arises.

You can help protect yourself by promptly contacting the supervisor who sent the letter and asking to see the compliance alert that prompted it. You may contact an investor claims lawyer who can contact the firm on your behalf. Understand that, once the hint of a complaint or inquiry is made, the representative from the firm will only want to protect the company's best interests, not yours. In my experience, supervisors are trained to deal with these calls by asking questions that are designed to create the impression that you are completely satisfied with your account's performance. Even seemingly innocuous customer comments are logged and can later be twisted by the brokerage firm's lawyers to their advantage.

Many investors make the mistake of calling their broker instead. Do *NOT* speak to your broker about the letter. I've seen many cases where customers do this and are tricked into thinking that everything is okay. Remember, if you've received a happiness letter, there's a good chance that something is seriously wrong. Don't give your broker the opportunity to talk you out of protecting yourself.

Finally, gather all the information you have about your investment account, including monthly account statements and trade confirmations, and seek the opinion of an attorney with significant securities arbitration experience. While Clark's and Edward's cases were some of the more dramatic results of cold-calling, I have represented many clients who were victims of the investment cold call.

Deception and manipulation are not straightforward endeavors. It's no longer enough to simply know the brokers you've hired and the tools they can access to betray you. To really safeguard your money, you need to know the investment products that can make or break you.

CHAPTER 5

___

Over Your Head and Under Your Radar

Truth be told, we need honest and diligent financial advisors. Most of us don't feel confident in our ability to design, implement, and manage a well-diversified investment portfolio on our own. We need an advisor's expertise to guide us, choose an appropriate investment strategy that meets our objectives and risk tolerance, implement the plan, and manage it.

In a perfect world, this would be a straightforward process:

- Do your research based on the tips and resources available in this book and hire an honest broker or investment adviser who is affiliated with a reputable financial services firm that has the necessary resources to adequately train and supervise its advisors.

- Meet with your advisor to discuss your specific circumstances, investment objectives, risk tolerances, investment experience, and particular goals.
- Rely on the experience, training, and expertise of the advisors and their firms to design, recommend, implement, and manage an investment portfolio that is appropriate and in the best interests of you and your family.
- Receive regular communication, information, and updates from your advisor who will recommend changes in your portfolio as appropriate.

Unfortunately, this professional process does not always happen. If you end up working with a bad advisor who purposely invests your money in overcomplicated or inappropriate products, the process can be overwhelming, with devastating results.

In this chapter, we'll discuss why some advisors use overly sophisticated products and steps you can take to avoid buying something you shouldn't.

NEVER OPEN A SELF-DIRECTED IRA

The securities industry is full of highly skilled people capable of designing and creating an almost unlimited number of sophisticated investment products that 95 percent of the general investing public have no business buying.

So why design such sophisticated products that only 5 percent of the population should actually buy? The keyword here is "should." The more sophisticated the investment product, the more money the securities industry and its sales force earns selling them.

Traditional IRAs, or individual retirement accounts, require a brokerage or bank custodian to hold and maintain them. These custodians are entities that have been approved by the Internal Revenue Service. Most IRA custodians limit the type of investments to stocks, bonds, mutual funds, and certificates of deposit.

A *self-directed* IRA is an IRA held by a custodian that permits investments in a broader set of assets than is permitted by most IRA custodians. Self-directed IRAs allow you to invest your tax-qualified retirement savings into alternative investments like real estate, promissory notes, tax lien certificates, and private securities. Investments in these types of assets carry a unique risk of fraud. Many of the widespread Ponzi schemes that I've witnessed in the last decade have profited from the use of self-directed IRAs. The reason is simple: most earners have their retirement assets grow in tax-deferred IRA accounts. If a schemers want access to that money by selling alternative investments that are not permitted in traditional IRS, they have to take the extra step of utilizing self-directed IRAs. All self-direct IRAs must be held through an entity called a "self-directed IRA custodian."

Self-directed IRA custodians are members of the security industry who are most susceptible to investor-defrauding schemes. Self-directed IRA companies specialize in unconventional investment vehicles—the very type of investment vehicles frequently utilized by fraudsters and scam artists. According to an alert on the Securities and Exchange Commission website:

> In particular, fraud promoters who want to engage in Ponzi schemes or other fraudulent conduct may exploit self-directed IRAs because they permit investors to hold unregistered securities and the custodians or trustees of these accounts likely have not investigated the securities or the background of the promoter. There are a number of ways that fraud promoters may use these weaknesses and misperceptions to perpetrate a fraud on unsuspecting investors.

Investments in these assets carry a unique risk of fraud. If opening a self-directed IRA is necessary for a particular investment that you are being pitched, take the advice of a long-time investment fraud attorney: don't invest. I strongly believe that retirees should avoid self-directed IRAs at all costs. Brokers will sometimes deceptively tell a client that the custodian investigates and validates the quality of the investments, giving the whole scheme an air of legitimacy. Most custodial companies are, in fact, legitimate entities, but the services they typically perform are limited to administration and record-keeping. They don't usually offer any real protection, despite what your broker may suggest.

I represented a group of investors working with a Ponzi-schemer using a self-directed IRA custodian called "Madison Trust." He named his fake investment scheme "Madison Timber," a scheme that cost investors $100 million. While Madison Trust and Madison Timber were completely unassociated, the similar names tricked investors into believing the legitimate custodian and the fraudulent scheme were affiliated.

DON'T BUY ANYTHING YOUR ADVISOR DOESN'T UNDERSTAND

Brokers and investment advisers have an obligation to understand the investments that they recommend. After all, how can they properly explain investments to their clients if they don't understand the investments themselves?

Many investment products are alternatives to conventional stock and bond investments. These products are sometimes referred to as structured products or non-conventional investments. More complex and typically riskier than traditional investments, financial advisors often sell structured products because they bring larger commissions than traditional investments. When the market is down or interest rates are low, investors are more susceptible to the pitches of better returns and alternative-product income. If your financial advisor pitches you products like high-yield or junk bonds, equity-indexed annuities, structured notes, private placements, leveraged- or inverse-exchange-traded funds, or reverse convertibles, I suggest avoiding them altogether but, at the very least, proceed with extreme caution.

In my experience, the vast majority of financial advisors who pitch these complex products don't understand the distinct features, risks, or investment strategies of the investments. Instead, they see promises of high yield and large commissions motivating them to sell. I only need a few minutes of their sworn cross-examination testimony in a case to establish that they have no idea what they're selling. And if they don't understand these investments, how can they properly explain them to their customers so that the customer can make fully informed decisions?

A private placement called "NGAS Partners" was once sold to Richard, a client of mine. Private placements are non-traded, illiquid securities offerings that are exempt from registration with the SEC and not subject to much of the regulations designed to protect investors. Richard's broker convinced him to invest a considerable sum in NGAS before it ended up going bankrupt. NGAS was a natural gas exploration company focused on unconventional operations in the eastern United States. The broker told Richard that he would receive excellent tax benefits with his NGAS investment and would most likely be able to sell it after three years for a nice profit.

I discovered in the purchase paperwork that Richard unknowingly signed it as a general partner instead of a limited partner, which explained the improved tax benefits. He had no idea that, as a general partner, he was personally liable for the debts of the company. If a natural gas well exploded and killed someone, Richard could be held legally responsible! When I cross-examined the broker at the hearing, he didn't think the heightened liability as a general partner was a cause for concern. In reality, I don't think he was even aware this was an issue for Richard. In the end, the arbitrators awarded my client exceedingly more money than he'd lost.

In a similar case, I represented Charlie, a 65-year-old brokerage customer from Texas. Charlie's broker talked him into investing his life savings in eight different high-risk private placements that were completely illiquid. Most of the investments involved oil and energy projects, and Charlie, a lifelong Texan, was a natural target.

Given Charlie's age and financial situation, investing in these risky placements was completely unjustified. Each private placement ultimately failed, and Charlie suffered substantial losses. Not only were these investments unsuitable, but the documents produced by the brokerage firm during the arbitration case proved that the brokerage firm and its co-owners responsible for performing due diligence failed to conduct meaningful analysis or investigation of the private placements before allowing their sale to customers. In fact, the due diligence files were completely empty. There was no possible way the broker or his firm understood these investments before they sold them to Charlie.

For the advisor, complicated private investments yield huge commissions compared to index funds or other investments more suitable for clients. It's a risky shortcut that some bad advisors are willing to take if they believe they can convince an unsuspecting investor that they know what they're doing, sell the product, and make it big. Like gambling, though, every detail must fall into place for success with these types of investments. The easiest part of the equation for the advisor is convincing the investor to buy the product. With products as complicated as private investments, most investors are satisfied knowing that they could make a solid return with dependable income. They believe their advisors know what they're doing. Often, this isn't the case. After seeing the devastating losses caused by private placements and structured products pushed on unsuspecting investors (typically retirees), my advice is to stay away from these complicated and risky investments.

VARIABLE ANNUITIES: ALWAYS SOLD, NEVER BOUGHT

At least twice a month, I receive calls from investors whose advisors have sold them variable annuities gone wrong. While I've never met an investor who sought to purchase an annuity, Americans invest approximately $100 billion annually in these products. I often say that annuities are never bought—they are only sold; customers only acquiesce after the advisor pitches the products.

A variable annuity is a contract between an investor and an insurance company. It's an investment account that includes particular insurance features, such as the ability to transfer an account into a stream of periodic payments or a death benefit. A variable annuity contract is secured through a single purchase payment or a series of purchase payments.

Variable annuity sellers excel at marketing, but their products require extreme scrutiny to decipher between the truth and fiction. As some of the most complicated products on the market, variable annuities are pitched by the advisor with glossy brochures featuring happy retirees enjoying their golden years on the beach. The explanation inside is oversimplified and generalized, often promoting a guaranteed lifetime income.

The contract itself, often nearly 200 pages or more, is riddled with opaque terms and conditions in small print that nobody reads. Hidden inside the pages are mentions of incredibly high contract fees and expenses, surrender charges that would reduce the value of the contract if you needed the money, and risk of loss. Truly understanding the annuities features requires a near-genius level of mathematical intelligence.

I can't tell you how many times I've called an annuity company with my client asking a representative to explain to us, in understandable terms, how the annuity's features actually work. It's a convoluted mess of guaranteed income payments that are not actually guaranteed, principal protection features that don't actually protect the principal, promised increases in benefit bases that arbitrarily stop, and invitations for guaranteed withdrawals that wipe out the fancy features investors have paid for. No one understands these "benefits"—investors or advisors.

One of the biggest problems I have with variable annuities is that they are typically sold to clients as a tax-deferred investment. "Tax deferral" means investments inside the annuity grow tax-free and taxes on gains are paid only as money is withdrawn. However, other investment vehicles—most notably IRAs and 401(k) plans—already offer tax-deferred growth. I've seen hundreds of situations in which advisors convince their clients to buy a variable annuity with money that is already in a tax-deferred account, like an IRA. You don't need the tax-deferred benefit of a variable annuity if your money is already in a tax-deferred account. It's crazy.

For retirees considering investing in a variable annuity in their IRAs or other qualified retirement plans, it's unlikely that the variable annuity will provide any additional tax benefits. A variable annuity only makes sense for these investors if the annuity's other benefits, such as lifetime income payments, are worth the cost. But for many investors, the costs usually outweigh the benefits. The expenses can easily bite off 4 percent or more of your account value per year. This means you need to achieve an annual return of 4 percent just to break even. Put another way, if the investments inside your variable annuity grow by 5 percent annually, your annuity is actually credited a meager 1 percent after expenses.

If your financial advisor wants you to invest your IRA money in a variable annuity, proceed with extreme caution. This is the bottom line: Having handled countless variable annuity cases against advisors, I think variable annuities are a bad fit for 95 percent of individual investors. Because the annuities are so complicated, it's nearly impossible to determine if you fall in the 5 percent of the population for whom they're appropriate.

One of the wildest annuity cases I've handled happened when a broker emailed his client (who eventually became my client) to "inform" him that if he invested $100,000 into a variable annuity that day, the value of the variable annuity was guaranteed to double in 10 years. After my client invested the money into a variable annuity, 10 years later to the day, my client contacted the broker requesting his $200,000. Of course, the extra $100,000 wasn't there. While salespeople will try to convince investors that a variable annuity will perform as well as the markets, they aren't accounting for incredibly high annual fees and their decimation of the annuities' value. In this case, I suspect the broker simply didn't understand what he was selling.

Most of the annuity cases I've handled have been against brokerage firms, but one of the most egregious cases involved a large, well-known bank. This case involved a young broker working at a local bank branch; this young broker struck up a conversation with the adult son of an elderly bank customer. The elderly woman had been a customer of the bank for more than 30 years and, at the time of the transaction at issue, was 82 and very ill. She lived in a nursing home and suffered from Alzheimer's disease, dementia, diabetes, blindness, and partial deafness.

In this woman's greatest time of need, the bank's broker tricked her family into liquidating several safe investments to pay a lump sum of more than $200,000 for an unnecessary and inappropriate annuity that would only pay the woman's beneficiaries 50 percent of the premium upon her death. Sadly, she died 15 days after the commencement of the annuity. The broker robbed this family's matriarch of $100,000 in the days and weeks just prior to her death. We sued the bank and won a full judgment in favor of my clients.

Most annuity cases that are referred to my law firm involve elderly clients. In a recent case, a broker took advantage of his position-of-trust with an infirm and senior customer by selling her a series of entirely inappropriate variable annuities. He directed his client to withdraw from existing annuities to fund the purchase of more annuities for no reason other than to generate additional commissions for himself.

Even more egregious, the broker manipulated his customer into signing the document stating that if she were to die before the commissions he was "owed" were fully vested and paid, he would be able to collect the annuity sales commissions from her estate. His client did die during this period, and he demanded $52,950 from her estate with a lawsuit. You can't make this stuff up.

Variable annuities also carry hefty surrender penalties, which apply to withdrawals made within a specified time period after the annuity is purchased. The penalty period is usually six to eight years, with some contracts extending 10 years or more. The penalty assessed is a percentage of the amount withdrawn and generally declines over time. For example, a 7 percent surrender penalty might apply to withdrawals made in the first contract year, then 6 percent in the second year. For investors who tie up their assets in a variable annuity and find themselves cash-strapped only a few years into the contract, surrender penalties can take a heavy toll.

Moreover, variable annuity contracts constantly change with insurance companies adding new and "dazzling" benefits touted as must-have features. In turn, this leads some brokers to recommend the liquidation of an older annuity that still has a surrender period and puts the proceeds—without the surrender penalty—into the new, supposedly better product. The advisor loves this because he's paid a large commission on the new sale. While regulators have cracked down on outlandish instances of exchanging annuities, it remains an industry problem.

VARIABLE UNIVERSAL LIFE POLICIES

Insurance companies have been selling an additional variable product that exists as the variable annuity's ugly cousin: variable universal life policies, or VULs. In my opinion, VULs are rarely, if ever, an appropriate investment choice. They're typically very expensive, offer poor investment choices, and fail to function as promised.

Like traditional life insurance, VULs provide a death benefit to beneficiaries in exchange for premium payments that are made on behalf of an insured person. But unlike traditional life insurance, the cash value in a VUL is invested in what are essentially mutual funds, with the cash value and death benefit rising and falling with the market.

In theory, this investment is supposed to result in a higher death benefit for beneficiaries because of better investment performance. But in most cases, VULs are loaded with fees and often fail to achieve a positive return.

In cases I've handled, investors are asked to pay significant upfront premiums or pay throughout the course of several years. They are assured that the VUL will ultimately pay for itself once the cash value grows to a certain value. This plan almost never works out as promised. Instead, after having dumped considerable amounts of money into the VUL, most investors find that the cash value fails to achieve sufficient returns to pay the premium. The investors must then deposit more money into the policy beyond the stated premiums, just to keep the policy afloat. More often than not, the investor finds that the VUL is simply unsustainable, and they have no other choice but to surrender the policy at a loss.

Sometimes, investors are told that the best way to maximize returns is to borrow money and use the borrowed funds for investment—almost always a bad idea for individual investors. Dave and Donna were clients who were talked into borrowing more than a million dollars for a VUL. After working more than 40 years running a family farm and scrap metal business, they decided to sell it and retire. Unfortunately, Dave and Donna were not sophisticated investors and never had significant investable assets. Selling their business and retiring finally meant they had enough money to invest.

They knew they needed help managing their money, so they met with a financial advisor they had known for years. In fact, their daughter even dated him in high school. Dave and Donna wanted to invest their money to generate income, and after several meetings with their advisor, he steered them into using their farmland as collateral to borrow more than $1.2 million for a grossly expensive VUL.

The policy came with hefty premiums that exceeded $38,500 every month as mortgage proceeds were deposited into a securities account with the advisor's brokerage firm and transferred to pay for the VUL premiums. Dave and Donna were assured that substantial cash values were building up in the VUL policies and that dividends being earned on the cash values would ultimately cover the premium payments. After nearly three years of dumping money into the VUL, however, the couple learned that their investment strategy wasn't working as promised. The mortgage proceeds in the securities account were eventually entirely depleted, and the dividends from the policies were not nearly enough to cover the hefty monthly premiums. To meet premium payments, Dave and Donna were forced to liquidate other investments. Ultimately, the premium payments were unsustainable, and the clients were forced to surrender the policies.

If your broker encourages you to borrow money to purchase an investment, recognize this as a glaring red flag signifying a dangerously unsuitable investment recommendation. While rare circumstances exist in which a very affluent investor may borrow money to boost investment returns, such a strategy is simply too risky for the average retail client.

One last thing about variable annuities (and any investment account or insurance product, for that matter): Make sure that your beneficiary information on file is accurate. Several years ago, I represented an elderly widow whose advisor failed to properly submit change-of-beneficiary forms for two different variable annuities for which she was the proper beneficiary. The widow learned about the broker's mistake only after her husband died and the annuity companies denied her death claims. Information on file with the annuity companies still identified the husband's estranged son as the beneficiary. Documents produced by the brokerage firm included copies of the change-of-beneficiary forms signed by the deceased spouse designating his wife as the proper beneficiary, but the annuity companies asserted that the forms were never received. As it turns out, the clients met with the advisor, the forms were signed, and the advisor said that he would send the forms to the annuity companies, but never did. The forms sat in the advisor's office for several years before they were found, and once they were located, it was too late. My firm was able to rectify the mistake and recover the money, but not without having to file arbitration claims against the brokerage firm and court claims against the annuity companies and estranged son.

DON'T LET YOUR BROKER PUT ALL YOUR EGGS IN ONE BASKET

It's one of the first rules for investors in the investment world: don't put all your eggs in one basket. In other words, diversify your investments. You may think this is fairly elementary, but you'd be surprised by how many "failure to diversify" or overconcentration cases I handle every year.

A diversified investment portfolio has a large mix of investments with different types of assets and industries. Diversification is a risk-management strategy that minimizes loss by following the understood rule that assets react differently to the same economic event. Portfolios should be diversified by asset class (stocks, bonds, commodities, and cash), by sectors, and by market capitalizations. If your advisor is not diversifying your portfolio, you, like many of my past clients, have a problem.

Prior to the 2015 energy market crash, the portfolios of many investors were filled to the brim with volatile oil and gas investments. Since the 2008 recession, the industry was booming, and brokers were selling their clients massive amounts of high-yield master limited partnerships and oil and gas private placements. As a result, investors' portfolios were overconcentrated in one sector and destined to fail with rapid changes in the energy markets. Unfortunately, that's exactly what happened. Between 2014 and early 2016, the global economy faced one of the largest oil price declines in modern history. We represented many investors suffering from the fallout for years following the crash.

Sometimes, the overconcentration isn't within an industry but within a particular holding itself. This happens when brokers are married to a particular stock, believe they know of something that could happen in the future, or own the investment in high concentrations.

One broker convinced Bill, a retired architect in Florida, to invest everything into a stock called Dendreon, a bio-tech company with a hopeful revolutionary immunotherapy product for prostate cancer. In 2009 and 2010, many believed Dendreon had the cure. Unfortunately, after Bill invested all his money in the company, Dendreon's stock value plummeted as the company abandoned its forecasted date for the release of the drug. Had Bill's investments been diversified, he would have avoided this extreme risk. Instead, he lost everything.

Similarly, we had a series of cases in which a broker talked his clients into investing in a gold exploration company based in Africa. The broker had more than a half-million dollars personally invested in it. He attended shareholder meetings, followed the company closely, and believed it was going to make him and his clients a good return. It's no surprise that brokers cannot give their clients conflict-free advice on a thinly capitalized stock that they hold themselves. Essentially, this broker could manipulate the stock price based on his recommendations to clients.

This is why it's so important to be wary of "hot tips." If brokers recommend an investment based on their own trading activity, fire them. Trust your instincts. You now know that diversification is important; stick to the facts when making investment decisions, no matter what your broker tells you.

Over the last several years, I've seen many investors have their portfolios wiped out by leveraged and inverse-leveraged products, including mutual funds and exchange-traded funds (ETFs). These products are basically overconcentrated positions on steroids. The goal of investing with leveraged funds is that they deliver multiples of a certain index performance or benchmark they track. For example, a leveraged S&P 500 fund may deliver a daily result of three times the total return of the S&P 500. The goal of investing with inverse funds, or "short funds," is that they deliver the *opposite* of the index performance or benchmark they track. Inverse funds often are marketed as a way for investors to profit from, or at least hedge their exposure to, downward moving markets. But too many times they are simply used by brokers to pump up portfolio returns in a last-ditch effort to achieve higher returns when an account is underperforming. I've seen many instances in which an entire portfolio is put into leveraged products, ending in disaster.

Heidi was one of my clients from California who ran a busy medical practice as an OB/GYN. Although Heidi considered herself a moderate risk investor, her broker took increasingly speculative positions in her portfolio. Nearly half of the portfolio was in one highly leveraged position as time went on. During a few short-trading sessions in 2015 when volatility suddenly spiked, Heidi's portfolio took a nosedive, and she suffered stunning portfolio losses of more than 85 percent.

I had another client endure a similar fate. Lauren had inherited a large sum of money from her father and saved all of it. Prior to turning 65, Lauren retired, believing she had plenty of money to last a long retirement. This would have been the case had she not met the wrong advisor who invested everything she had in a variety of leveraged ETFs. Lauren's portfolio was wiped out in a matter of a few months.

Neither Lauren nor Heidi understood the exceptional risk their financial advisors took with their investments. In both cases, the financial advisors were smooth talkers with polished sales pitches, and the leveraged investments were sold to my clients as tools to help hedge or mitigate risk. If my broker started talking about "leveraging," I would treat it as a warning and start looking for a new broker. Never have I encountered a scenario where clients have benefited from holding leveraged positions in their portfolios.

SECURITIES-BASED LENDING: IT PAYS TO SEE BEYOND THE PITCH

Any time advisors suggest you borrow money for a future expected return in your account, you can guarantee their goal is to leverage the loan for *their* benefit, not yours.

Trading on margin is when a customer borrows money from a firm to purchase securities. The loan is secured by investments purchased by the customer, with the customer paying interest on the margin loan. Advisors recommend margin to their customers to increase the customers' purchasing power. The securities industry can sell more investments and earn more commissions—or fees—with margin trading because the customers are able to buy more securities.

As a general rule, the customer's available cash in the account must not fall below 25 percent of the current market value of the securities in the account (for example, $25,000 in cash with a portfolio value of $100,000). If the value of the portfolio declines, the customer is required to deposit more funds to maintain the equity at 25 percent. If the customer cannot deposit more money, the firm will force the sale and liquidate the securities in the customer's account to bring the account's equity back to the required level. The firm doesn't even have to contact investors to make such a liquidation valid. You can lose more money than what you initially deposited if the value of the securities sharply declines. This is a strategy that unsophisticated and risk-averse investors should never use, yet it happens all the time.

Another securities-based lending product that is a key revenue source for brokerage firms is the Securities-Backed Line of Credit (SBLOC). Firms use these in times of solid market returns and growing investment portfolios when investors feel more comfortable leveraging their assets.

Essentially, this is a loan that customers take from a financial institution using the assets in their investment portfolio as collateral. In contrast to margin, which can only be used to purchase securities, these loans can be used for a variety of expenses, including college tuition, vacations, home improvements, and living expenses. Investment portfolios can be bought or sold as usual, but investors must keep a minimum value to the portfolio, per their collateral pledge agreement. Brokers who sell their clients on an SBLOC often earn additional compensation or a portion of the fees generated from the SBLOC.

SBLOCs carry enormous risks. As we ended the longest bull market in history in 2020, sharp volatility in virtually all asset classes had caused a wave of margin and maintenance calls. As the value of pledged collateral decreases, investors are expected to come up with the money, or their investment positions may be liquidated.

For most investors, coming up with the money to quickly pay off an SBLOC is not an easy task. The typical investors using an SBLOC have spent the money on something that is not easy to sell or cannot be returned, like a house or college tuition payments. In this case, investors may suffer substantial losses as a result of forced liquidation of their investment portfolio, the underlying collateral. Forced liquidations can also result in substantial tax liability for which investors are often unprepared.

I represented a gentleman in Louisiana who sold his ranch and intended to use the cash to fund the construction of a new home for retirement. His broker learned of the sale and convinced his client to deposit the cash into his investment portfolio and take an SBLOC out for his new house. The interest rate was good, and the broker promised my client he could earn more on the money than interest would cost. Once my client agreed, the broker put that money almost exclusively in the oil and gas industry. The sharp 2015 market declines decimated my client's portfolio and forced him to sell the house he had just built in order to pay off the loan.

Investing on margin is essentially gambling. No one except experienced traders should borrow money to invest, least of all anyone retired or close to retirement. The benefit to brokers is that their commission sharply increases if their gamble—with your money—is successful. If it isn't successful, you pay with your investment and interest charges.

You've now seen the bad and the ugly of the brokerage world, but remember that most brokers and investment advisers are, in fact, good. Still, the chaos and destruction that the bad ones cause make exposing them in arbitration and court one of the most fulfilling parts of my career.

In Part 3, I'll show you how to trust your gut. It may be trying to warn you that a battle is brewing.

If Something Goes Wrong, You'll Need a Lawyer—a Great One

As you can see, investment misconduct can blindside you. Other times, it's hard to tell if your investment losses are the result of your advisor's misconduct. I turn away far more cases than I take, but even when I cannot represent investors, at least I can help them make sense of the chaos.

If you've been harmed by your advisor's misconduct, the sooner you find an experienced investment fraud lawyer to fight for you, the better. The securities industry can be an overwhelming foe. It's the most well-financed industry in the country, with near-endless resources and sophisticated defense lawyers. You deserve to match the industry in strength—a battle against Wall Street requires an army.

In Part 3, we'll explore how to find the most qualified investor claims lawyer for your case, how my legal team evaluates and accepts representation of these cases, and the stages of the legal process for recovering investment losses.

CHAPTER 6

———

Is There a Problem?

No one wants to be a victim. We like to believe that we're in control and that we have the power to change a bad situation and make it right. But the quicker you regain your composure after learning that you may be a victim at the hand of a bad advisor, the closer you are to recovering your money.

Some investors can be tricked for years to believe that everything is fine with their investment account, making it that much more of a humbling experience when they realize their money is gone. It's often not until they request access to their money or seek the advice of a trusted advisor that they notice something is wrong.

NOTICE THE SIGNS

No matter how long you've worked with an advisor, it can be

difficult to spot the signs that your investments have gone south as a result of misconduct by your advisor or financial firm. Following are a few clues that it's time to look for an experienced investment fraud lawyer.

LARGE FLUCTUATIONS IN YOUR INVESTMENT PORTFOLIO

Investments that take a sharp dive can easily capture investors' attention. But when investments spike upward quickly, we're less likely to be concerned or ask questions. We may even praise our broker. But if an investment gains a steady return month after month in a time when the market is experiencing significant fluctuations or is otherwise flat, this could be a sign of a problem. Any large fluctuations in your investment—in either direction—should prompt you to ask questions. Even if your broker has an explanation that sounds reasonable, contact their supervisor and request a meeting to review your account. It never hurts to have more information, and if something is wrong, the sooner you catch it, the better.

SUDDEN CHANGES IN YOUR ACCOUNT ACTIVITY

Whether you receive electronic or hard copies of your account activity every month, ideally you should take the time to review these statements yourself and never rely on a statement your broker personally provides. Account activity varies from investor to investor, but once you've established a baseline for "normal," it's ideal to keep an eye on your statements to make sure there are no sudden changes, such as a flurry of trade confirmations or large movements in or out of a particular investment strategy. I say "ideal" because life often gets in the way, making it unrealistic to do a deep dive into the specifics of the account holdings. In my experience, most investors focus on the bottom of the first page of their account statements where it reports the total account balance. They rely on their advisor and firm because the account specifics are difficult to understand.

NO CONTACT WITH YOUR ADVISOR

You should be able to reach your advisor with any questions or concerns in a reasonable timeframe. If you try to contact your advisor, and they are consistently unavailable or fails to return your calls, you can bet there's a problem with your account. Also, if your advisor is evasive when you ask questions and doesn't give you straight answers, this is another red flag.

Other signs of a problem with your advisor include high-pressure sales tactics, promises of no risk or minimal risk, excuses for not being licensed, or the promotion of unregistered investments.

WARNING: SIPC PROVIDES LIMITED PROTECTION

When investors lose money in their brokerage accounts, many mistakenly assume that stock or bond losses due to inappropriate investments or negligent account management are covered by the Securities Investor Protection Corporation (SIPC), a nonprofit created in 1970. This is incorrect. The SIPC provides limited coverage for an investor's brokerage accounts when the firm has failed or is in danger of failing, or when there are losses from unauthorized trading or theft.

When a brokerage fails, most clients' securities are held by clearing firms and remain perfectly safe. Membership in SIPC is mandatory for brokerage firms and clearing firms that pass trades for broker-dealers. Since the financial crisis of 2008, SIPC has been involved in the Lehman Brothers bankruptcy and the Bernard Madoff Ponzi scheme debacle.

There are monetary limitations on damages that clients of SIPC members can collect. SIPC protection limits are capped at $500,000 for missing stocks and other securities, including $250,000 for cash held in certificates of deposit, money market mutual funds, and the like. Customers of SIPC members are covered for losses up to these limits.

WHAT SIPC DOES NOT COVER

SIPC provides protection in certain situations but does not provide protection for any decline in value of securities between the time a firm goes out of business and the time claims are processed and approved. They also do not provide protection for clients who are sold worthless stocks and other securities, or for bad investment advice or unsuitable investments.

As you can see, SIPC offers protection to investors when their broker's business fails or is in financial trouble, but that protection has major limitations and doesn't cover most circumstances. If you have losses that result from other situations—poor account management, unsuitable investments, or outright fraud—you need to pursue formal legal recourse through an experienced investment attorney.

DON'T TRY TO WORK IT OUT ALONE

When investors are convinced something is wrong with their investment, they often go directly to their financial advisors. It makes sense—you've trusted them this far; surely you can trust them now to explain the issue. But it's rare for the bad actors to come clean and make it right at the outset. And if they do try to pay you off to settle the complaint without their firm involved, they create a host of potential issues.

First, financial advisors are not allowed to simply reimburse you out of their own pocket for any wrongdoing on their part in an attempt to wash their hands of the ordeal. Specific regulatory disclosures must be made the second you lodge a complaint against your advisor. Any advisor who tries to pay you under the table is flouting these rules.

Second, investment loss analyses are complicated and usually require a forensic expert to unpack. When financial advisors attempt to give a client money to fix the problem, the offer is usually not even close to the sum the investor lost from the advisor's actions. It may tempt you to take the money and run, but the offer is likely a small fraction of your actual losses.

You may think that your next step is to contact a supervisor at your financial advisor's firm. This also sounds like a reasonable idea, but understand that from the moment you lodge a complaint with supervisors, their firm goes into protection mode and they immediately become your adversary. Simply put, they want you to go away for the least amount of money possible and will never make a sincere effort to help you understand the problem or what happened. Instead, they'll defend themselves by pointing out the reasons they want you to believe you're wrong and offer a small portion of your losses in return for you sacrificing your rights to make a future claim against them.

If you do make a complaint on your own, you may receive a letter from the firm suggesting they conducted a "thorough" review of your complaint and found no wrongdoing on their part. I've seen hundreds of these "denial" letters from firms to their customers. They're written from an employee of the firm with a fancy title like "Compliance Manager" or "VP of Operations" and often full of one-sided details designed to convince the clients that the firm devoted significant time and resources determining that their brokers did nothing wrong. I can almost repeat, verbatim, the contents of these letters from memory.

In my experience, these denial letters serve one purpose: to convince the client to drop the complaint and not hire an investment fraud lawyer to pursue their claims. Don't fall for this trick.

If you find yourself at this point, you need an ally and advocate. You need a lawyer who devotes their legal practice to investment fraud and can tell you if you have a case and what that case is worth. Most of us in this line of work will provide free case consultations. You have nothing to lose and everything to gain by consulting a good lawyer.

CHAPTER 7

———

You Can Win the War, but You'll Need an Army

For the last 25 years, I've built an army in my law firm to represent victims of investment fraud. With more than 1,000 clients represented and $350 million recovered, my team and I have unearthed a number of truths along the way:

- Too few know about investment fraud and the destruction it can cause in its victims' lives.
- Financial advisors have an advantage over their clients. They can choose to use the trust that their clients have placed in them and work with integrity, as most do. But they can also choose to violate that trust and leverage their clients' investments for personal gain—and they

might get away with it. Fortunately, law firms like mine are stopping their advance.

- Too many people struggle to find the right legal team to represent them. You don't want a lawyer who lacks the necessary experience, credibility, resources, and firepower. I guarantee you that your opponent, the Wall Street firm, will not hire just any lawyer with the lowest fee and shiniest website.

I know how frustrating it can be to sift through lawyers' advertisements and websites because the internet makes it hard to tell the difference from one lawyer to the next. As with many industries, the internet has made everyone an expert in something. It's important that you take the time to pull back the curtain and make sure that the lawyer and the legal team you hire will truly level the playing field in your fight against Wall Street.

HOW TO FIND THE RIGHT LAWYER FOR YOU

As we've discussed, it's difficult to find lawyers whose specific focus is investment fraud. A few more of us exist now than when I started in 1999, but true expertise in this area of the law takes a long time to build. There are no shortcuts. At my law firm, we have the benefit of more than 20 years of legal experience specific to investment fraud, investment products, and investment firms, including the rules and laws that govern them. Most importantly, we know how to take cases all the way to trial—and win. I have consistently been voted by my peers as a "Best Lawyer" by *The Best Lawyers in America®* publication, and my firm has been peer-voted as a Tier 1 Best Law Firm© for many years.

Remember that your advisors are supported by their firms, and their firms are supported by Wall Street lawyers with near-limitless budgets. To make this a fair fight, you need the best legal team you can find.

Your legal team's resources matter to you in the long run. Most investment fraud lawyers are contingency fee lawyers who advance case expenses like filing fees, expert witness fees, and travel expenses. Almost all plaintiff lawyers say that they work on a contingency fee basis, but truly having the financial resources to cover all upfront costs of a trial or arbitration for multiple clients is a separate matter. If an investor loses half a million dollars and hires us, for instance, we may spend anywhere from $10,000 to $75,000 or more in out-of-pocket expenses in case preparation. These are expenses we absorb if we fail to recover our clients' money. The impact of expenses on the legal team you select ultimately impacts you. Expert witnesses, for example, are usually necessary to win a case but come with a hefty price tag. Often, the best experts are extremely expensive and are selective in the lawyers with whom they choose to work. These experts can cost $100,000 or more.

The harsh reality is that selecting a solo practitioner or small firm with inadequate resources based on a flashy website alone can have a devastating effect on how your case turns out. If you hire a lawyer with a caseload of 100 clients, do they have the financial resources to pay more than $500,000 in advance for case expenses? If not, you can bet they'll be forced to cut corners or work the case "on the cheap" because they don't have sufficient resources to handle the case properly. With one chance to recover your money, you can't afford to take a chance with an underfunded or ill-equipped legal team.

AN ARSENAL OF RESOURCES AND EXPERTISE

Fighting investment fraud is the foundation of my law firm. Our six lawyers and 10 support staff have substantial arbitration and trial experience. We have strong relationships with experts who have the experience and aptitude for working on big cases. With two lawyers assigned to every case, each client receives exceptional attention. Our robust legal team devotes extensive time, energy, and resources to review thousands of documents, research arbitrators, write comprehensive legal briefs, consult the best experts in the business, prepare comprehensive exhibits, and present the best possible case to the arbitrators or jury.

The relationships of mutual respect that we build with defense lawyers, arbitrators, and mediators are enormous assets we can't put a price on. These are the career-long relationships that help cases get resolved for our clients on terms that are fair and just. For example, many of our cases are resolved through settlement in mediation prior to the final hearing or trial. We have a handful of mediators in the country with whom we regularly work. It's important to cultivate relationships with the mediators built on mutual respect and regard.

RECOVERING YOUR INVESTMENT LOSSES

Most people have, thankfully, never been involved in a lawsuit. The majority of our clients have never experienced a legal proceeding, so we make sure they are well-informed on the timeline and proceedings of their case. Let's now walk through the steps of recovering your investment losses.

Evaluating a Potential Case

The proper and diligent analysis of a potential case is a critical part of the investor claims process. Many lawyers advertise on the internet that they provide a "free case review." At my law firm, this is a much more extensive process. With a full-time case analyst who has worked at my firm for 18 years, we take claims analysis to a different level. We're comprehensive in approach, especially compared to other firms that offer a 10-minute phone call with a paralegal or a lawyer taking the call on a cell phone while attending to 10 other matters at the same time.

Much of my time is spent analyzing potential investor claims and figuring out whether I can help an aggrieved investor. There's no "one-size-fits-all" approach to case evaluation. It's a fluid process that may take weeks of collecting and evaluating investment documents before we make a decision. Other times, I know immediately, without looking at a single document, that the investor likely has a great case. Before we can help a client, we must address four factors:

- *Are there investment losses?* Sometimes, investors call us when they're upset about a particular fee structure or misrepresentation that they believe was unfair and actionable. While we may agree that the investors didn't get great service or the best possible price, unless they have suffered actual financial losses, there's not much that can be done in pursuing a legal claim. A viable legal claim is only actionable once damages are suffered.
- *Is there misconduct?* Not every investment loss is the result of fraud or the sale of an inappropriate investment. All investments necessarily carry some risk of loss; for the most part, the differentiator between appropriate risk and actionable wrongdoing is in determining whether investments are correctly matched with an investor's risk profile and investment objective.
- *Is there a viable defendant?* In Part 1, we discussed the

various ways to determine the financial viability of an investment firm. This analysis becomes very important for this step. Occasionally, over the course of my career, I have won cases against firms with brokers who undeniably caused significant losses but never paid a penny. Instead, they went out of business or filed bankruptcy. It's heartbreaking to represent clients from the beginning to the end of a case, win, and never be able to recoup their losses.

- *In what forum would we have to bring this claim, and do the amount of damages justify the costs involved?* When we file a case, we pay filing fees, forum fees, and expert fees, with some forums more expensive than others. For example, if the agreement you entered in with your investment adviser specifies that any dispute will be brought in a private arbitration forum, I immediately know that the case must be large enough to balance out the forum expenses. In most private arbitration forums (excluding FINRA), I cannot bring a case worth $75,000 because, even if we win, the forum's fees could be more than the losses recovered. Conversely, the expenses in a FINRA arbitration case tend to be much lower, and they have a simplified arbitration process designed to accommodate smaller cases. My law firm advances expenses in the vast majority of our investor claims cases but, if we are successful in recovering money, those expenses are reimbursed. This is why we must determine, at the outset, if the losses justify the potential costs incurred.

We dig deep into analyzing the potential clients' account statements and investment documents to evaluate whether they have valid claims. We have potential clients shipping us countless boxes of account statements and emailing us dozens of messages and account material. Since we have a deep bench of professionals with many years of experience evaluating potential claims, we're able to invest the time and effort potential clients deserve so that they receive a complete, honest, and accurate analysis of their potential claim and whether there's a case to pursue in the first place. If we discover a strong claim, we extend an offer to represent you on a contingency fee basis. We only earn a fee if we recover money for you.

Filing the Legal Claim

All account-opening documents at brokerage firms and other financial institutions contain what is called a mandatory arbitration provision. This provision requires that any dispute that customers have against a broker or brokerage firm must first proceed through arbitration and not a court of law. Securities arbitration is a highly specialized area regulated and administered by FINRA. The rules and procedures for pursuing a case in FINRA arbitration are very different from filing a case in court. Just as rules of civil procedure must be followed in court, an entirely different set of rules and procedures exist in FINRA arbitration.

One of the many differences between FINRA arbitration

and court cases is that rather than filing a complaint to initiate a court case, the document filed with FINRA is called a "Statement of Claim." Some lawyers file short statements of claim for their clients simply to establish the case, but I've found that our clients are better served by researching, preparing, and filing a robust statement of claim. Of course, it takes more time and resources to prepare a comprehensive filing that outlines the factual and legal basis to support the client's claim. I want the arbitrators who are ultimately appointed to my client's case to know from the outset, though, that we're taking the matter seriously and pursuing a legitimate claim worthy of their time and attention.

Selecting Arbitrators

The arbitrators selected in a client's case will have the same power that a judge and jury would have if your case was filed in court. Selecting arbitrators is a crucially important part of any investment fraud case. Our legal team works hard to see that the most qualified and fair arbitrators are selected to decide each case.

For cases filed against brokers and brokerage firms in FINRA arbitration, FINRA maintains a database of thousands of arbitrators trained and approved by FINRA to serve in customer disputes. After a case is filed, FINRA generates a random list of arbitrators from its roster, sending the list to attorneys for both the customer and the brokerage firm.

Under FINRA's rules, counsel for the parties is then permitted to strike a certain number of arbitrators from the list and rank the remaining arbitrators in order of preference. The parties submit their ranked choices to FINRA confidentially—neither knows who the other party struck or how they ranked the arbitrators. FINRA combines the parties' ranked lists and seeks to appoint the highest-ranked available arbitrator from each list to serve on the panel. For cases involving damages of more than $100,000, three arbitrators are selected. Smaller cases are decided by a single arbitrator.

Our law firm maintains comprehensive research files on numerous FINRA arbitrators throughout the country. We learn where they went to school, their employment history, and how long they've been arbitrators. Our records contain every prior FINRA arbitration decision made by these arbitrators, and we track their decision history both in actual dollars awarded and as a percentage of the dollar amount sought in each case. We don't rely on just the information disclosed by the arbitrators themselves. We dig deeper, gleaning information from publicly available resources that give us insight into the arbitrators' backgrounds.

We also draw upon our personal experience with many arbitrators, noting which ones are more likely to run a fair hearing and give the parties a fair opportunity to present their case.

The Discovery Process in FINRA Arbitration

After a FINRA arbitration case is filed, it proceeds to the discovery phase. It's during this phase that parties work to obtain facts and information from the other parties in the case to support their claims and defenses in preparation for the final arbitration hearing. FINRA has specific rules governing the discovery process, including how to make, respond, and object to discovery requests, and how to resolve discovery disputes between parties. This includes issuing sanctions against parties for discovery abuses.

With discovery requests, FINRA has declared that certain documents are presumptively discoverable in all customer disputes. This includes a list of documents brokerage firms are expected to produce in customer disputes, as well as a separate list of documents that investors are expected to produce. Such documents include new account forms, contracts signed by the customer, notes maintained by the broker or brokerage firm, emails between the parties, and the customer's tax returns.

When it comes to responding to discovery requests, a party may object to a request if it asks the party to provide documentation that a party believes is, for example, overly burdensome, irrelevant, or involves confidential or privileged information.

If the parties cannot agree on their own how to resolve any

discovery dispute, the party who still wants more documents may make a motion to compel the reluctant party to produce the requested information. The arbitrators may schedule a hearing before deciding the motion. If a party fails to produce documents required by a discovery order, the arbitrators may issue sanctions against that party. Sanctions could include assessing fees or penalties, prohibiting a party from introducing evidence at the hearing, or even dismissing a claim, defense, or entire case.

Mediation

When our team obtains the documents and evidence necessary to build and present a case, we consider whether the case is a good candidate to be resolved, or settled, prior to the final arbitration hearing. In our law practice, we have found great success in resolving many of our clients' claims through a process called "mediation."

Mediation is a voluntary process that takes place on a parallel track with your pending FINRA arbitration case. Parties agree to work with a neutral, professional third-party mediator who doesn't work for either the investor or brokerage firm. Instead, the mediator's job is to work with both sides in an effort to settle the case.

If done properly, mediation offers a degree of control and predictability. At mediation, the parties are active participants and have real power in working toward an acceptable outcome. On the other hand, at the final arbitration hearing, all parties are subjected to cross-examination and the panel of three arbitrators makes a decision that is binding and impossible to predict.

Mediations typically take a full day and are held at a mutually agreed upon location or virtually via Zoom. Sometimes they begin with a joint session during which the mediator explains the process, and parties may highlight some of the key arguments supporting their positions.

Following the joint session, parties usually move to separate caucuses. Mediators spend time separately with both sides talking confidentially about the strengths and weaknesses of their evidence and their legal positions. Throughout the day, mediators work with the parties and exchange offers, counter-offers, questions, demands, and proposals between both sides to help the parties move closer to resolution. All communication with the mediator is confidential, and they may not share any information without permission.

The mediator has no authority to decide the settlement or even compel the parties to settle. Mediation is non-binding and completely voluntary. If it's a success and the case settles, the final hearing is canceled, and the settlement is consummated within a few weeks. If the case doesn't settle, it proceeds to a final hearing with arbitrators.

The Final Arbitration Hearing

While many of our law firm's cases settle through mediation prior to an arbitration hearing, there are certain instances when the parties aren't able to agree on a resolution. Not all cases are appropriate for mediation or settlement. When this happens, parties present their case to the arbitrators and let them make a final decision. The proceedings in a FINRA arbitration are similar to the proceedings in other private arbitration forums used by investment advisers, such as the Judicial Arbitration and Mediation Services (JAMS) or the American Arbitration Association (AAA).

While an arbitration hearing is less formal than a court proceeding, the process resembles a trial that you've probably seen before on TV. Since cases are not filed in court and not decided by a judge or a jury, they are not conducted in a courthouse. Rather, the final hearings are typically held in a conference room. Even though the hearing setting is less formal than in court, nobody should be fooled: the arbitrators' decision following the final hearing is binding for all parties, and the available grounds to appeal a FINRA arbitration ruling are extremely narrow.

At the start of the hearing, all parties, counsel, and arbitrators are gathered in the conference room. The lawyers for each side begin by making opening statements to the arbitrators. These are intended to give the lawyers for the parties the opportunity to summarize their client's case and what they intend to prove at the hearing. After opening statements, the investor's lawyers present their case-in-chief, when they call witnesses to testify under oath in response to questions under direct examination, followed by the opportunity for the brokerage firm's lawyer to ask questions of the witnesses under cross-examination. Once the investor rests their case, the roles reverse, and it's the brokerage firm's opportunity to present its case. As before, witnesses are called and subject to both direct examination and cross-examination under oath.

Typical witnesses in a securities arbitration case include the investor, the broker who advised the investor, the broker's supervisors, and expert witnesses who may provide testimony about damages calculations and standards of practice in the securities industry. Most of our law firm's arbitration hearings last about three or four days, but some complex cases may last longer. Throughout the arbitration hearing, the parties may object to particular evidence or lines of questioning and the arbitrators must decide whether to sustain or overrule the objections. While the formal rules of evidence don't technically apply in FINRA arbitration hearings, most arbitrators are lawyers and they rely on the rules of evidence as a guide when evidentiary disputes arise.

Once the parties have presented their evidence, each side has the opportunity to make closing arguments to the arbitration panel. This is when lawyers summarize the evidence that was presented and provide their arguments for why the evidence supports their case and why the arbitrators should rule in their party's favor.

Presenting a persuasive case to a FINRA arbitration panel involves tremendous amounts of preparation, strategy, research, and expertise.

After the hearing is over, the arbitrators meet privately to review the evidence and make their final decision. Following FINRA's rules, the arbitrators must issue their decision within 30 days of the final hearing date.

After the Final Hearing

If a case proceeds to a final FINRA arbitration hearing and the panel rules in the investor's favor, the investor receives an arbitration award. Once an award is issued, it must be paid by the responsible party within 30 days of the issue date of the award.

FINRA coordinates with its dispute resolution and enforcement programs by verifying whether a firm or broker has paid an award on time. If the respondent has not paid, FINRA initiates suspension proceedings. If the respondent doesn't pay the award, they will not be able to continue operating as a broker or brokerage firm.

FINRA arbitration awards are final and are not subject to

review or appeal unless the broker or firm has filed a motion to vacate or modify the arbitration award in a timely manner under the applicable laws. Although standards differ slightly across the country, FINRA arbitration awards are typically only vacated or modified in rare circumstances, such as if the award was procured by fraud or other serious arbitrator misconduct.

The laws regarding arbitration awards differ among jurisdictions, but a major benefit of the FINRA arbitration process is that, typically, if the case is decided in favor of the claimant and the brokerage firm is in business with the financial ability to pay, the claimant receives payment in accordance with the issued award very quickly. Likewise, if the investor doesn't prevail in the arbitration hearing, the opportunity to appeal the adverse decision is likely very limited.

THE BIG PICTURE

Case outcomes are important, but representing the interests of the investing public to the best of our ability is at the forefront of everything we do. A safer, more secure investment landscape isn't easy to achieve. Every year, with an organization of other investor-protection attorneys, I travel to Washington, D.C., to meet with Congress and federal regulators and push for legislative and policy changes to enhance investor protection.

There's still work to do, and for every inch forward, a seemingly unshakeable wall of industry lobbyists try to block our progress. But it's a fight worth fighting. Our clients need their voices heard and the chance to reclaim their lives. They can't accomplish this without us, a fact that my office takes very seriously. It's a great privilege to be our clients' advocates and to know that the time, effort, and resources we dedicate to their cause can change the trajectory of their lives. It's not just about their lives, though; it's also about their legacy.

Conclusion

Accepting my first case of investment fraud when I was 28 was the best decision of my career. After dedicating decades to help these victims in their fight, I've found that the real requirement for an investment fraud lawyer is the right combination of passion and compassion—the passion for aggressively and strategically fighting for clients and the compassion for understanding why clients hire us in the first place. I firmly believe that my firm has achieved this important balance. After all, we understand that it's not just about lost money. It's about everything else lost along with it.

It's also about the shame and embarrassment harbored simply for trusting that people will do what they say they will. It's about working and saving, anticipating and planning, only to have a cheater take a shortcut and destroy everything.

It's about the challenges of growing old and losing cognitive function, and people seeing this loss as their gain.

This is why I fight. And it's why you should fight, too.

We all benefit from taking the time to ensure we're working with people we trust, especially when so much is at stake. No one in a professional position should have a history littered with unethical actions and still be in business. The more we expose the true intentions of bad brokers, the closer we are to living in a world where we can trust others and invest safely.

If you're already a victim of investment misconduct, you can't take any chances. The legal team you hire must be trustworthy, knowledgeable, and successful. This advisor must be passionate *and* compassionate, ready for a challenge, and able to anticipate obstacles. Most importantly, the lawyer must have a long track record of winning.

No systematic hurdle or Wall Street defense stands a chance against an experienced legal team fighting for the ultimate prize: their client's redemption.

Your legal team is the one shot you have to get everything back. Don't waste it.

I invite you to contact me directly if you have questions about the topics covered in this book. You can reach me through my law firm's website at www.investorclaims.com, by email at dmeyer@meyerwilson.com, or by telephone at 1-800-738-1960.

Acknowledgments

First, I want to thank all of my clients who entrust me with their important cases, as well as their attorneys and other trusted advisors who refer my clients to me for representation. I feel like I am the most fortunate lawyer on the planet. I get to go to work every day and advocate for the most deserving, hard-working people who are depending on me to fight to restore their financial security while holding the powerful Wall Street firms accountable.

The secret to my success is really no secret at all. It's my team at Meyer Wilson. In my opinion, they are the best in the business. My law partner, Matt Wilson, is one of the smartest people I have ever met. He was the first in his family to go to college, and he attended on a full academic scholarship. After graduating from one of the top 10 law schools in the country, he went to work as a corporate litigation defense attorney at one of the largest law firms in the world. I am not sure how, but in 2006, I convinced him to quit the fancy Big Law job and join me fighting the good fight. Fifteen years in, and I could not be prouder of the law firm we have built together.

Two other attorneys at the firm helped me with this book. I want to thank Courtney Werning and Chad Kohler. In addition to the help on the book, they are with me in the trenches every day as part of our Investor Claims Team, and both are excellent trial lawyers. Paralegal Beth Robertson and Claims Analyst Adele Hyde are also critical members of our Investor Claims Team. I want to thank attorneys Michael Boyle and Richie Clark for their great legal work. Our legal team is also supported by paralegals Aaron Porterfield, Kemmily Kwok, and Jamie Kendrich, and I am grateful for their commitment and service to our clients. The entire operation runs smoothly thanks to the tireless efforts of my longtime office administrator, Tiffany Rucker. She has my back 24/7.

A special thanks to my parents, Stephen and Lynn Meyer, and Phyllis Sopher. You always believed in me and supported me, and for that, I am grateful.

And, most importantly, I'd like to thank Melora, my biggest fan. She didn't intentionally marry a plaintiffs' trial lawyer, but to her credit, she supported me every step of the way and was the constant rock through plenty of rough seas as I worked to get the law firm off the ground years ago. When I completed the first draft of this book, she dove right in with her signature purple editing pen (she never likes to grade her students' papers with red ink). I was struggling with one paragraph in particular, and, when I asked her for her insight, she read closely and wrote, "You can do better." So I went back to work. Thank you, Melora, for pushing me to be better.

About the Author

DAVID MEYER is the managing principal of Meyer Wilson, a national law firm he founded to represent investment fraud victims in their fight against deceptive brokers. Meyer Wilson is one of the nation's leading investment fraud firms, recovering millions of dollars for clients throughout the last 20 years. David is currently the president of two bar associations: the Public Investors Advocate Bar Association and the Ohio Association for Justice. Included in *The Best Lawyers in America*®, David has also been twice named "Lawyer of the Year" by the publication in his practice area and location. For more information about David's investor claims law practice, visit investorclaims.com.